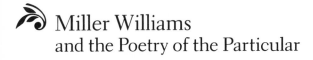

Miller Williams
and the Poetry of the Particular

Miller Williams
and the Poetry
of the Particular

Edited by Michael Burns

University of Missouri Press
Columbia and London

5 4 3 2 1   95 94 93 92 91

Library of Congress Cataloging-in-Publication Data

Miller Williams and the poetry of the particular / edited by Michael Burns.
    p.   cm.
  Includes index.
  ISBN 0–8262–0807–X (alk. paper)
  1. Williams, Miller—Criticisms and interpretation. I. Burns, Michael.
PS3545.I53352Z74   1991
813'.54—dc20   91–20227
                                                                        CIP

∞™This paper meets the requirements of the
American National Standard for Permanence of Paper
for Printed Library Materials, Z39.48, 1984.

Designer: Elizabeth K. Fett
Typesetter: Connell-Zeko Type & Graphics
Printer: Thomson-Shore, Inc.
Binder: Thomson-Shore, Inc.
Typeface: Elante

A *Poem for Emily*

Small fact and fingers and farthest one from me,
a hand's width and two generations away,
in this still present I am fifty-three.
You are not yet a full day.

When I am sixty-three, when you are ten,
and you are neither closer nor as far,
your arms will fill with what you know by then,
the arithmetic and love we do and are.

When I by blood and luck am eighty-six
and you are someplace else and thirty-three
believing in sex and god and politics
with children who look not at all like me,

sometime I know you will have read them this
so they will know I love them and say so
and love their mother. Child, whatever is
is always or never was. Long ago,

a day I watched awhile beside your bed,
I wrote this down, a thing that might be kept
awhile, to tell you what I would have said
when you were who knows what and I was dead
which is I stood and loved you while you slept.

 Contents

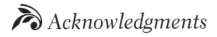 *Acknowledgments*

I am especially grateful for the patience and support of my family—Vicki, Shannon, and Dakotah—as this book was coming together. I also want to thank my colleagues at SMSU who listened and advised. My very special thanks to all of the authors who contributed their essays to this collection.

Selections from the poetry of Miller Williams and his translations from Belli are used by permission of Louisiana State University Press.

Translations from Nicanor Parra are taken from *Poems and Antipoems*, copyright 1967 Nicanor Parra. Reprinted by permission of New Directions Publishing Co.

Part One of Howard Nemerov's "Looking Forward, Looking Back" appeared originally as the introduction to Williams's *A Circle of Stone* and is reprinted by permission of Louisiana State University Press. Copyright 1964 by LSU Press.

"Out of the Hills of Certainty" by Fred Chappell first appeared in *The Cotton Boll/Atlanta Review* and is reprinted by permission of the author. Copyright 1989 by Fred Chappell.

"Tradition and Personal Vision" by Lewis Turco first appeared, in a slightly different version, in *The Hollins Critic* and is reprinted by permission of the author. Copyright 1989 by Lewis Turco.

"To Advantage Dressed" by David Baker first appeared in *The Southern Review* and is reprinted by permission of the author. Copyright 1990 by David Baker.

"Miller Williams, Translator" by R. S. Gwynn first appeared in *The Translation Review* and is reprinted by permission of the author. Copyright 1989 by R. S. Gwynn.

"The Sanctioned Babel" by Richard Jackson is reprinted by permission of the University of Alabama Press from *Acts of Mind, Conversations with Contemporary Poets*. Copyright 1983 by The University of Alabama Press.

"A Descriptive Chronology" by Lyman Hagen appeared, in an earlier version, in *The Bulletin of Bibliography* and is reprinted by permission of the author. Copyright 1987 by Lyman Hagen.

ix

Miller Williams
and the Poetry of the Particular

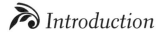 *Introduction*

Michael Burns

Over the past twenty-five years, Miller Williams has published eight books of poetry, culminating in his recent *Living on the Surface: New and Selected Poems,* for which he was awarded the prestigious Poets' Prize for 1990. The publication of this significant body of work enables us as careful readers to begin to answer the questions that arise from our reading. They are standard ones: (1) What have been the poet's central concerns? (2) what forms has the poet chosen for conveying these concerns? (3) out of what tradition, or in response to what personal influences, has the poet developed his work? (4) how does his poetry compare or contrast with the work that has been done or is being done by his contemporaries? and (5), to use Helen Vendler's words, what "imaginative claim" has the poet "staked out" as uniquely his own? The essays collected here, though not asked to address these questions specifically, do begin to provide answers.

Part I is composed of essays that focus on the poet's central concerns. What better way to begin than with the "before and after" remarks of Howard Nemerov, who has known Williams and his work for the span of his career? He tells us that Williams has been "growing and staying the same," "keeping the delicate balance between faith and the sardonic." Fred Chappell examines how, when Williams's poems take up philosophical questions, he uses "the hypotheses and conclusions of contemporary science" and thus demonstrates a "pervasive and enduring skepticism." Like most of us, Maxine Kumin has her favorite Williams poem. Her discussion here is primarily a close reading of "Why God Permits Evil," which she says forces us "to see past the banality of the question into the humble human search for eternal verities." In the final essay of this section, William Stafford offers us a short, lighthearted appreciation of the pure pleasure of Williams's poetry, where "what blights a life must be faced down with clarity, irony, humor, tenacity."

1

Most of the essays in Part II respond to questions of form and influence. X. J. Kennedy's "The Poetry: Form and Informality" covers a wide range of Williams's poems in traditional forms, from the couplet to the quatrain, the sonnet to the sestina. Lewis Turco, in his detailed explications of whole poems and parts of poems, shows how "form helps the poet to say the necessary thing." In their essays on the dramatic monologue, John Frederick Nims and C. D. Wright demonstrate how, in his use of this venerable form, Williams makes it his own. Tracing the roots of the monologue from Browning through Frost, Nims examines eight of Williams's recent monologues, noting with pleasure and anticipation that "a poet with nearly three decades behind him is finding fresh territories to explore." Wright takes her cue from the fact that Williams is the son of a Methodist minister to suggest that it is Williams's "rootedness in religion which bestows upon his monologue an abiding treelike nature." David Baker's essay, "To Advantage Dressed," concludes this section with a slightly different emphasis. Discussing the various rhetorical methods poetry may employ, Baker compares and contrasts Williams's strategies with those of other important poets of his generation, specifically that group of writers identified with Stephen Berg and Robert Mezey's anthologies *Naked Poetry* and *The New Naked Poetry*.

The essays in Part III also provide answers to questions about Williams's poetry, but they take a more personal approach. R. S. Gwynn recalls the early days of the translation workshop at the University of Arkansas, and he focuses on Williams's work as a translator, especially of the Chilean poet Nicanor Parra and the nineteenth-century Roman poet Giuseppe Belli. Gabrielle Burton's "Of Devils and Saviors" describes her first encounter with Williams at Bread Loaf in 1972. James Whitehead's essay brings the collection to a close. His recollection of a trip he and Williams took together from Nashville to Columbus, Mississippi, in 1958 gives insight into the times and forces that shaped the young poets.

Finally, Part IV provides readers with a chance to listen to Miller Williams talking about his craft in an insightful interview with Richard Jackson, while Lyman Hagan's "Descriptive Chronology" presents a biographical and bibliographical summary.

So we arrive at the end of this collection with question number 5 only indirectly answered. In scholarly terms, it may be the hardest of questions, but I believe the answer is here, whole in the sum of the parts. This is a poetry of the particular, and many who know Williams and his work will already have answered the question for themselves. John Ciardi, shortly before his death in 1986, addressed it in a way that sets the stage well for the discussion to follow:

> Miller Williams writes about ordinary people in extraordinary moments in their lives. Even more remarkable, doing this, is how perilously close he plays to plain talk, without ever falling into it; how close he comes to naked sentiment, without yielding to it; how close he moves to being very sure, without ever losing the grace of uncertainty. Add to this something altogether apart, that what a good reader can expect to sense, coming to these poems, is a terrible honesty, and we have among us a voice that makes a difference.

I.

A Poem for Emily

My very darling, we are ~~separated~~ set apart — I am fifty three —
by two generations, which is the way
— considering the one between us — it ought to be.
~~I am fifty three. You are a day~~
~~You have not what~~ yet a full day —

When I am sixty three and you are ten
~~I'll~~ and you have known me since the world began
~~and I have taught you~~
~~I'll teach~~ ~~tell you what I~~
~~I'll ask you'll tell you~~
~~I'll tell you I~~ ~~being ten~~
I'll ask you ~~who~~ what you know when you are ten
perhaps, you'll teach me what you've learned by then
~~and~~ and ask me things I'll tell you if I can.

When I am eighty nine years old and you
are thirty six and have ~~perhaps~~ some ~~kids~~
who look ~~not much like me~~ as are a two
are thirty six and ~~have a colleen~~ years?
at least and ~~are~~ are married
~~and have a~~ ?? as have one or two
~~children who don't look~~ I ~~have a~~ at
children who ~~don't look like~~ at all like me
look nothing

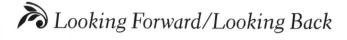 *Looking Forward/Looking Back*

Howard Nemerov

Foreword to A *Circle of Stone* (1964)

These poems, built of the simplest materials, appear at first to be simple themselves; simple and impenetrable, as the observation of life has a way of being. Some of them are simple (or continue to appear so after several readings), for example, "On the Death of a Middle Aged Man." Something about the voice, as well as the preoccupation with death as the one revealing situation, reminds us of Edgar Lee Masters (to my mind not a bad place to begin considering poetry), but this voice is more impersonal than Masters's, more sardonic, and less exclusively conditioned by social considerations, which it usually transcends to arrive at a desperate wrestling on metaphysical grounds, where a religious sensibility and a scientific training dispute, generally on questions of sexuality and death. Even in the poem about a man misfortunately named Beverly, there are a couple of items suggesting a deeper design; if you put together the marvelous offhand remark about Helen, who with a couple of no-count exceptions "never did nothing / Christ would have died for," with "A minister who didn't know him either / said he was forgiven," you seem to penetrate a touch further into the sense of the poem—a sense that gets one further horrifying twist in connection with the boy named as a girl when you realize that the conventional "bosom of Abraham" has suddenly got a literal sense; the heaven referred to, even if it did exist, would be an androgynous monstrosity.

There is sometimes an awesome rightness to these poems, especially to their endings, where terrible suggestions, older than meaning, half-emerge from darkness. I am far from being able to "explicate" all that I feel in the finish of the poem "For Robert, Son of Man," but I can say what I feel in the strange image of

> a circle of stone
> where the sun slips red and new
> to a stand of oak.

I hear an echoing inter-allusive whisper about Stonehenge, the sacrifice of Isaac, and circumcision, and feel this in the context of the poem as absolutely just; "the sun *slips* red and new" (where the adjectives insist you read also "son") seems to me a passing marvel.

Admittedly it is a marvel many readers will pass without remarking. Admittedly also, it is possible I am wrong; nothing so unusual in that, either. But I get a certain quantity of confirmation from the way in which Miller Williams's poetic preoccupations support and go with my reading of those lines.

Another poem that has this rightness, at once simple and inexplicable, is "Depot in a River Town." You read it first as a description; very well, you've been in a station yourself, you know how it is. . . . Then you begin to be preoccupied with a certain ritual effect secured first by the heavily swinging alliteration of the repeated line, "In the depot and the darkened day." Maybe then you notice the curious insistence on religion and art in the figures "like a child in church," "like a nun telling beads," "after an ancient painting." Then you see—I am attributing my own experience of the poem to a generalized Reader—that the detail about the fog is more than picturesque; you are to infer that the trains are not running. Having got so far, you are in a position to contemplate the last strophe: the trains that are not running would run along the river; the river is, as traditionally, the time-stream; the journey to be taken is across the river, perpendicular to, hence out of, time; the penny is to pay Charon. But the poem has never said so—all that comes up as a slow, not unconsoling revelation closely related to sleep.

It may be said that I am being too ingenious (though not so very ingenious even so). It may also be said that poems demanding ingenuity are bad, or "out," or whatever. To which I can say only that I prefer poems that want to be read hard and that respond to the closest attention. Sometimes I wish Miller Williams would be rather more explicit; at other times I delight in his slight deviousness which knows more than it says aloud. This is not a matter of depth of thought, for to the sophisticated intelligence of this poet who knows how to be simple in the word no thought will be shallower or deeper than another; it is a matter rather of how you approach one thought through another, how one thought steps from behind another with an effect of surprise; a matter of the steepness of the gradient between the immediate and the inferred.

Not everything here has this distinction. Sometimes he is affectedly melodramatic—as at the end of "June Twenty"—and a few of the poems are "merely" imagist notes. But it is remarkable how much he gets in of the agonizing complexity of the human response to life, to situations that are simple only because they are also impossible; remarkable how sensitive his language is to the ultimate identity of hope and hopelessness, of sarcasm and tragic resignation, of social protest and religious abandonment to despair. This balance is explicitly discussed in "The Associate Professor Delivers an Exhortation to His Failing Students," where the failure on both sides is set against the scientific or theoretical probability of the failure of the human entirely (according to the best of our knowledge, we never *did* come down out of the trees); and all this balanced with the minimal hope at the end that Prometheus ("some impossible punk") will, or did, anyhow, bring down fire from heaven. And the torn, suffering nature of his response, explicit in that poem and more or less so in one that balances it, "Notes in a Minister's Hymnbook," turns up tightly and cryptically dramatized in some of the finest short pieces, "For JW, on his marriage in the faith," "On the Slaying of a Music Student in Philadelphia by Teenagers," "To an Idealist Sitting In," and "Wait for the Wagon." The last two especially just because of a certain cruelty, just because they hurt, are poignant and necessary lessons to the liberal intelligence about the savage humility that must inform any attitude to evil, if good is to come in the end.

· · · · ·

A year or more before I wrote the above Foreword, at Bread Loaf when Miller was nominally my pupil but really already my instructor, we were walking through the woods when he pointed out a nail driven laterally into the trunk of a young pine about four feet from the ground. "How high do you suppose that nail will go in twenty years?" said Miller, and I replied with the arbitrary confidence of extreme ignorance: "Seven feet." "No," said Miller, "it'll still be right where it is." I've always remembered that, and now it comes in handy, for Miller and I make our parables sometimes of such trivial-seeming things.

Thinking of my friend's distinguished career over the more than two decades since that walk, I think to put together the pine and the nail, the right answer and the wrong one, the letter and the allegory, to note that Miller's poetry has been characterized by the reconciliation of those two opposite or discordant qualities, growing and staying the same.

While continuing to find his subjects in the daily ordinary everywhere around him, Miller seems to see ever more deeply into them; volume by volume, his work shows a steady increase in definition, seriousness, and terse eloquence; keeping the delicate balance between faith and the sardonic that was already so evident to me in A *Circle of Stone*, he has gained in concision and wit, a gain that shows also in his translations from Giuseppe Gioachino Belli and Nicanor Parra. For a short instance, consider "People" from *The Boys on Their Bony Mules* (1983):

PEOPLE

When people are born
we lift them like little heroes
as if what they have done
is a thing to be proud of.

When people die
we cover their faces
as if dying were something
to be ashamed of.

Of shameful and varied heroic things we do
except for the starting and stopping
we are never convinced
of how we feel.
We say oh, and well.

Ah, but in the beginning
and in the end.

That one is on my (very) short list of lifetime favorites, for it is with discovery in poetry just as Albert Szent-Györgyi said it is with discovery in the sciences: looking at what everyone has looked at, seeing what no one has seen.

I think I spoke accurately of Miller's work in that Foreword to his first collection, and I'm happy to see it reprinted in this celebration of his growing-and-staying-the-same. And I'm honored at having our long friendship do the same.

Miller Williams's Skeptical Science
Fred Chappell

Miller Williams has produced some of the genuinely humorous poems of our time, along with some of the most passionate love lyrics, in colloquial language of fine nuance and hard power. But when his poems turn to large philosophical concerns they are likely to employ the hypotheses and conclusions of contemporary science, as well as its terminology, in order to reveal the poet's pervasive and enduring skepticism.

The paradox inherent in this method, this usage of the language of precision and certainty in order to exhibit and explore Williams's distrust of impersonal data and of all generalization, is entirely in keeping with his insistent playfulness, his thorough questioning of the value and purpose of intellectual striving. Williams's attitude toward intellectual endeavor is largely ambiguous, but perhaps it could be formulated in crude terms in the following sentence: Man can never know truth but he is damned if he doesn't try to; and damned also if he does try.

A more graceful presentation of some aspects of this skepticism is the epigrammatic poem "It's Hard to Think the Brain":

> It's hard to think the brain
> a ball of ropey dough
> should have invented pain
> or come to know
>
> how there are things we lend
> a fragile credence to
> and hope to comprehend
> but never do.

Williams repeatedly advances the notion that the objective truths we think we have discovered by dint of determined effort are only constructions of the mind, ideations that may amount to no more than subjective fantasies. In "Some Lines Finished Just Before Dawn at the Bedside of a Dying Student It Has Snowed All Night," he throws doubt on the prevalent concept of a four-dimensional space-time continuum:

> Some physicists believe in four
> planes of space. This is more
> than we can know, lacking the sense
> to see the plane our reason bends
> about the other three. This
> is not called faith. That's what it is.

It is called, of course, not faith but science. But since this scientific construct depends entirely upon something, a fourth dimension, that the senses cannot apprehend, it is an object of faith. God, too, is an object of faith, the poem goes on to say, so why shouldn't we believe in God? Come to that, why shouldn't we believe in any object of faith?

> And cherubim and seraphim?
> Ghosts and ogres? Vampires? Elves?
> People who can turn themselves
> to cats and make potatoes rot
> and curdle a mother's milk? Why not?

In this poem Williams rages at the limits of knowledge because they limit the range of the speaker's sympathies. He cannot enter into the dying student's experience; he cannot imagine what the experience must be like, and compares the failure of his imagination to a dimming light in which subjective phantasms are glimpsed.

> Already the light when I turn that way
> is dim. Sometimes I see the shapes
> of people flying. Or clouds, perhaps.
> Or trees. Or houses. Or nothing at all.

The feeling of drained helplessness that the speaker articulates in this poem is found in many of the poems that deal with the problem of knowledge. In "The Associate Professor Delivers an Exhortation to His Failing Students" the speaker is possessed by such a thorough skepticism in regard to the possibility of knowledge that he comes near to despair. He warns his students about "getting hung up in the brain's things / that send you screaming like madmen through the town." He claims that any girl "anonymous as beer" encountered in a bar could have taught his subject as well as he. He avers that "there is no Jesus and no hell," that "all the answers at best are less than half." He advises his audience that their surest hope is to abandon hope.

> The day I lectured on adrenalin
> I meant to tell you
> as you were coming down
> slowly out of the hills of certainty
> empty your mind of the hopes that held you there.

Miller Williams seems at first glance willing, and even anxious, to push an unnerving skepticism to the limit. He shows little faith in scientific method. The laboratory frogs the associate professor refers to in his exhortation are regarded as having given their lives "for nothing" and "are washed from the brains and pans / we laid them in." In his most ambitious essay at the problem, the long poem called "Notes from the Agent on Earth: How to Be Human," he refers to the scientist as "the pither of frogs and cat-slitter." And the characterizations of scientists throughout his poems show them as confused, depressed, despairing, or even, in one teasing love poem ("The Assoc. Professor [Mad Scientist] to [His Love] His Student in Physics 100 Lab"), as crazy.

It is not only scientific knowledge that Williams lacks faith in. Philosophy and art are equally untrustworthy. In "The Proper Study" the practice of introspection as the method of the mystic, the psychologist, and the philosopher is seen as presenting us only with phantasmagoric and meaningless images in place of truth, "a blue anteater with seven heads," for example, and an "aged mother / rocking in her lap a pig." But when the seeker turns his attention outward, when he investigates the objects of nature as an astronomer, he finds after staring at a star with his "biggest telescope" that "it's not a star, it's not a star, it's a hole!" Both methods of investigation yield up either illusion or disillusion.

In the poem "He Speaks to His Arguing Friends and to Himself" the discussion shifts to ontology. "There is no question / except the question of final cause." The poet considers two possibilities, the first being that the universe came into being ex nihilo, from "pure unplace." He cannot bring himself to believe this notion. "This is one impossible road." The other impossible road is to believe in God. "Imagine a mind that always was, / where *In the beginning* makes no sense. / Think it thinks us into being." The speaker finds neither alternative convincing. "Either way you'd bet not."

Even so, even though he is faced with two impossibilities of which neither offers advantage over the other, the speaker chooses between them; he chooses to believe in God. His choice seems at first glance a resigned one caused by what William James referred to as "failure of nerve."

> But we have believed through such pain
> and made such music for so long
> that it would be a hurt and shame
> if we should learn that we were wrong.
> We have enough to fret about.
> Almost all of us concur,
> we'll live with the holidays we have
> and the grace of God as if it were.

Yet the choice here is not resigned or arbitrary or cynical; it proceeds from a different but closely related current of Williams's thought, a strand of his thought that is concerned with the nature of systems and with the possibility of affirmation.

The first alternative offered us in "He Speaks to His Arguing Friends" is not the old-fashioned one of creation happening merely by means of utter chance. Williams refers instead to the very recent idea that nothingness is in itself a creative force, that it is actually in the nature of the void to give rise to physical being. He describes this "pure unplace" in witty terms, then says, "Imagine that it all explodes / (although there's nothing to explode) / till matter and energy come to be."

Williams's grounding in science, whether it is a professional technical grounding or not, looks to be pretty thorough and up-to-date. New theories amuse him and sometimes bemuse him, and he handles them with ease and often with relaxed humor. Perhaps he is able to do so because he puts so little faith in them as final answers; in fact, he would seem to wish to reject final answers even if they could be found. Perhaps he imagines for mankind the happy destiny of never making a conclusive choice among metaphysical possibilities. In one poem he congratulates the euglena, that unicellular flagellate that biologists classify sometimes as a plant and sometimes as an animal, for evading the definite choice of phylum and surviving because of that evasion:

> Fencerider,
>
> you've held your own for twenty
> million years

who might have been a tulip
or a tiger

you shrewd little bastard.

If neither philosophical introspection nor scientific investigation can provide absolutely certain data, if final metaphysical choices ought to be evaded or selected for the sake of human convenience and spiritual comfort, then not much is left objectively to believe in, except for that one organ or faculty or talent which enables us to believe—that is, the mind itself. There is a constructivist flavor to Williams's thought; he may owe more than has been remarked to Alfred North Whitehead. We make up our minds about reality and, having done so, have made up reality.

Williams likes not only to compare but to equate the so-called objective nature of science and the subjective nature of poetry. In an early poem, "Level IV," he takes the physicists' definition of "work" as a definition of poetry: "there is a change / in temperature." The associate professor in his fervid exhortation makes the same kind of comparison between science and poetry.

The day you took the test
I would have told you this:
that you had no time to listen for questions
hunting out the answers in your files
is surely the kind of irony
poems are made of

Not only is one intellectual system as valid as any other in this benevolent skeptical view, they are all equal in purpose, method, and result; they are interchangeable in terms of a grand algorithmic superstructure. The terms of metaphor—that is, of analogy—are not only interchangeable, in Williams's view, they are interdependent. In his poem "Form and Theory of Poetry" the pattern of traffic around a football stadium at game time is used to describe the thermodynamic career of a hurricane. Then the analogy of the hurricane is used to describe the complex motions associated with a football game and its spectators. "Form and Theory" is a curious, centerless poem that arouses in a reader an odd relativistic sensation because neither term of the metaphor is stable. An ordinary poetic metaphor will compare this girl here and now to that rose there and then; one term is taken as literal, the other as imaginary. In Williams's poem both terms, football game and hurricane, describe one another interchangeably; both terms are simultaneous and timeless at once; both terms are literal and imaginary at once.

> Think in the eye of a hurricane, then, of Tittle,
> Thorpe and Namath, Simpson, such acts of God.
> At a football game, think of the gulf coast,
> Biloxi, Mississippi blown away.

This relativism of analogical terms enables widely disparate systems of thought to illuminate, illustrate, and validate one another because it makes them all equal as metaphoric terms in poetic structures.

This idea is dealt with more explicitly in "Believing in Symbols," which advances the proposition that all intellectual ideas are derived from a single idea. Williams's image for this notion is the number 8 as we find it in the display of a digital calculator. The speaker of the poem has put a calculator into the pocket of his shirt, over his heart, where it has shorted out. "That afternoon / it lay on my desk and turned out 8s for hours." He considers them as two symbols, the calculator representing science, the heart representing emotional life or the life of the spirit: "So what do we say for science and the heart? / So with reason the heart will have its way?" He then makes a humorous point about this Pascalian dichotomy and passes on to ponder, in the second half of the poem, the nature of symbols.

All the numbers, "1 through 7, also nothing and 9," can be formed by lighting up portions of the two stacked squares that compose the digital 8. This 8 is "the figure all the figures are made from"; it is "the enabling number, the all-fathering," although (and also because) it "is only itself." He finds other likenesses for the number—the self-enclosing single-surfaced Möbius strip, and the sidewise 8, ∞, which is the mathematical symbol for infinity—and in these guises too the 8 is "all-fathering."

The succession of digital numbers inside the framework of the 8 reminds the speaker of successive eras of history, which also take place inside an inescapable frame. "The pterodactyl, Pompeii, the Packard; / things take their turns." Numbers that once held mystic and religious meanings are seen to be only emphasized parts of the one superstructural figure; "3 and 7 are only / numbers again." Looking back to his calculator/heart symbolism, he characterizes historic eras as being dominated either by reason or by emotion—and then declares that the opposition between the rational and the irrational is specious, and may even be illusionary.

> Not to say that physics will ever fail us
> or plain love, either, for that matter.
> Like the sides of a coin, they may take turns,
> or flipping fast enough, may seem to merge.

The poem next pursues the image of the flipped coin spinning in the air. The dichotomies melt together; heads or tails, reason or unreason, it all amounts to the same thing. It is a game of chance. However you think about reality, your terms are equally correct and incorrect, equally viable and equally useless. Whatever terms you may invent are inadequate and inapplicable. When you gamble by flipping a coin you lose because you call heads but tails comes up. In Williams's game you lose because heads-or-tails doesn't matter; heads is wrong, and tails is wrong too.

> Call it, if you call it, in the air.
> When the coin comes down, the tent comes down.
> You look around, and there is nothing there.
> Not even the planets. Not even the names of the planets.

Every shred of certainty is stripped away—the science that discovers the planets, the history and mythology that are employed to name them. The traveling carny game is over; the tent comes down.

The poet's conclusion is a bleak one for those who have put their faith in the spurious declarations of philosophy and science. Any truth that was ever gained is interchangeable with any other truth; all is relative. In "Notes from the Agent on Earth: How to Be Human" Williams finds another image (it is a variation upon Lucretius's illustrative argument for an infinite universe) for the relativistic point of view. The undefined place where each of us stands seems to someone else a well-defined horizon.

> What matters most in survival is learning the names
> of things and the names of visions. If the horizon
> for an example were real someone could go there
> and call back to the rest of us and say
> Here we are standing on the horizon.
> But he would see that his friends were standing on it.

Yet the vision is not entirely cheerless. This stanza about the relative horizon begins with an affirmative statement: "There is much that matters. What matters most is survival." And, after considering the relativistic paradoxes of space-time, the poem examines our attempts to avoid the bitterness of the paradoxes by means of self-induced illusion and then adjures us to eschew illusion so that we may attain the primary value of survival. The memories we keep of time past "are illusions, or seem to be illusions. / Leave them alone. What matters most is survival."

Miller Williams belongs to that class of poets who feel compelled to tell us things they know we are not eager to hear. Lucretius is a poet of this sort, and so are George Crabbe, Thomas Hardy, and Robinson Jeffers. Yet, if we could be persuaded to give up our illusions, they seem to say, there might be some point in our vain hopes, in all our earnest fruitless striving.

The poem "Entropy" may be understood to set forth this position. The first four sentences describe in thoughtful and humorous metaphors and images the relentless consequences of the Second Law of Thermodynamics, but the final two words of the poem may allow our efforts and hopes a glimmer of legitimacy and efficacy. "Intend," says Williams twice, echoing in striking fashion the final injunction of Robert Frost's "Provide, Provide," and echoing too Frost's grim tone. The imperative here exhorts the friends to give their greetings with all purposeful good will, with genuinely amicable feeling. Even if nothing is accomplished, even if everything must expire at last, it makes a difference for us to mean well toward one another and toward existence as a whole. The blind scientific facts that make up the universe will not be changed by even our best intentions. But our best intentions are admirable and make a difference in the complexion that can be put upon things. So Miller Williams implies in this poem, and if this thought is not the happiest a poet has ever brought to us, it is as sanguine as this unflinchingly tough-minded poet can make it.

ENTROPY

You say Hello and part of what you spend
to say it goes to God. There is a tax
on all our simplest thoughts and common acts.
It will come to pass that friend greets friend
and there is not a sound. Thus God subtracts
bit by little bit till in the end
there is nothing at all. Intend. Intend.

 *Who and Where We Are*

Maxine Kumin

Some jacket-copy writer, who deserves to be known and praised for it, said of Miller Williams's seventh book, *The Boys on Their Bony Mules*, that his poems "Believe . . . in saying who we are before we are nothing." I admire that statement for its plain speech, its unadorned truth, and the bravery it reflects, all of which shine in Williams's work. From the beginning I have been attracted to the cadence of his poems, the country rhythm of his diction, the seemingly direct frontal approach he takes to an often slithery subject, the way the language disarms the reader and then sneaks metaphysically behind him/her.

As a stunning example of this poetic truth and treachery in one, let me take my all-time favorite Williams poem, "Why God Permits Evil: For Answer to This Question of Interest to Many Write Bible Answers Dept. E–7." The epigraph to this ponderous title tells us it was found on a matchbook cover but in no way prepares us for the dips and swoops of thought we are about to embark on.

As if by contrast to the simplistic formulation in the title, Williams begins by alluding to Calvin, Aquinas, and Job, all of whom find this question "of interest." None receives a straight answer, though Job "gets his cattle back. / With interest." Do we remember, reading this, that at the end of his torment Job is rewarded (by what has always seemed to me a very materialistic Yahweh) with exactly twice as many animals as he lost—fourteen thousand sheep, six thousand camels, one thousand yoke of oxen (which comes to two thousand animals), and one thousand she-asses, let us pray that none of these is barren?

So Job gets his livestock back with interest, "which is something, but certainly not / any kind of answer." Here the poet shifts into direct address: "unless you ask / God if God can demonstrate God's power / and God's glory, which is not a question."

It is of course the eternal question, eternally unanswered except by faith. Initially it is not clear whom the poet is addressing; is this aimed at his audience? I am caught and implicated here, only to discover from the succeeding strophes that Williams has each of his exemplars in mind. "You should all be living at this hour," he declaims, paraphrasing Wordsworth's apostrophe to Milton, a sonnet composed in London in 1802 that calls on the long-dead poet to rescue society from its stagnation and moral torpor, heightened for Wordsworth by the recent revolution in France and its subsequent overthrow.

Now we are raised to that pitch and let drop. Calvin, it is said, "had Servetus to burn" at the stake for his heresies in 1553, and the doctrines contained in the *Institutes* to write, chief among them the notion of divine election that ghosts us still. Aquinas had his Latin, "the hard bunk and the solitary night," which hardly measures up theologically to the attention paid Calvin. Perhaps this says something about Williams's heritage as the son of a Methodist minister. And Job's ordeal is reduced to the bad advice of his neighbors, and his wife "yelling at you to curse God and die."

Biblical, literary, and philosophical allusions often prove a difficult gristle for the contemporary reader to chew on, but they are invaluable for thickening the authenticity of the poetry of ideas. The range of them seems narrower in contemporary poetry, as does their comprehension. But even the reader who may not understand most, or indeed any, of the allusions cited is teased along by the forward movement of the poem. "Why badness makes its way into a world He made?" rephrases the question stated in the title in very much the colloquial tone I have come to associate with Williams's work. It is harder than it looks.

Even as we know the question to be unanswerable, we are drawn further into the internal argument, into the stark contrast Williams poses between Job, Calvin, and Aquinas on the one hand, all of whom had faith and endured in spite of anguish, and "we" who "have E-7." Yet the teasing suggestion is made that there is little difference between the simplism of a mail-order assortment of answers to the unanswerable and the absolutism of faith in the unprovable. This kind of spinning out to the edge of rationality is characteristic of Williams's work. He is a realist, using a Rouault-like hard outline to make his point, then veering at what is the last possible moment away from the precipice.

There are two notable hairpin turns in this poem. The first comes with the establishment of the regular iambic pentameter line (though the opening foot is trochaic) that will carry the poem from here on:

> Some place on the south side of Chicago
> a lady with wrinkled hose and a small gray
> bun of hair . . .

Here at last, breathes the reader, cometh revelation. But no. Instead we have more questions, more departments, even departments dedicated to hair-splitting, as in the question of whether animals have souls.

And just when we expect—no, demand, "beyond the alphabet and possible numbers"—an answer, the poem makes another sharp turn to deliver the final evasion by way of another image. This one is arranged to oppose the first. Here we have "a pale, tall and long-haired woman / upon a cushion of fleece and eiderdown" who stuffs answers into envelopes. We will never learn the substance of these, for there is no substance. Like a koan asking what the sound is of one hand clapping, the image evanesces and we are left with our nonanswer in a silent room behind a door that never was.

The appeal of the poem lies in its very brashness, in its holding out in the most provocative manner a promise it will never deliver, thereby forcing us to see past the banality of the question into the humble human search for eternal verities. Nowhere in Williams's poems do we get the dispassionate, disinterested kind of statement that was the hallmark of George Bernard Shaw, who could pronounce, for example, about death: "It is a fact like the rising of the sun and has simply to be faced, not argued about." Blessedly, Williams is an arguer. The poetry is in the argument. He is not a moralist, but his poems set out almost invariably to follow the spoor of a moral trail. He says who we are, then asks what we might have been.

This stance comes clear in two poems that quite purposefully abut each other in *The Boys on Their Bony Mules*. One, an elegy for Victor Jara, the musician who was tortured and then murdered in the debacle that followed the overthrow of Salvador Allende in Chile, asks how far any of us would have borne witness in that political climate. Would we have "stayed to the end," "or would we have folded our faces?" Williams draws no conclusion; he simply says "you have embarrassed our hearts."

In "Wiedersehen," Williams again makes the process of identification and empathy highly personal. A memoir of German prisoners of war in a small town in Arkansas being driven in an open truck past a group of adolescent boys who have been playing baseball, the poem charms us in low key. On impulse the persona, presumably Williams himself, tosses his friend's baseball to one of the prisoners, "A boy barely older than I was and blonder." The whole team races down the road after the truck in pursuit of the now-lost ball; at the last moment the German winds up "and let[s] the ball / fly in a flat arc from center field." The poet then considers this particular German, wonders "if he had killed the Rogers boy / or thrown the hand grenade at Luther Tackett / that blew his arm away."

These are acceptable if predictable musings, given the historical backward thrust of the poem. But then, set apart in a concluding couplet, Williams writes:

> Your grandchildren, German, do they believe the story,
> the boy in Arkansas, blonder than you?

Let us hope so. The way Williams transforms the trauma of World War II into a salvageable anecdote does not diminish the past. On the contrary, it heightens it by making it accessible. I am reminded of Hardy's poem "The Man He Killed." It concludes:

> Yes, quaint and curious war is!
> You shoot a fellow down
> You'd treat if met where any bar is,
> Or help to half-a-crown.

Williams's work as I read it is very much of a piece, wry, skeptical, pitying, and above all persistent in proclaiming that "something such as we are will scurry on," that human rituals, however impoverished or incomplete, are "still one way of knowing where you are."

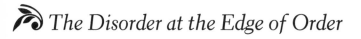

Robert Wallace

THE WELL-ORDERED LIFE

Once he went inside a pool hall.
The clicking billiard balls put him in mind
of African tribes who click to say, "I love you"
"What do you want?" "We're going to kill you, of course."
They skirted the circles of light in a secret frenzy.

He took his Instamatic every week
and thirty-five dollars to life class.
He didn't use film. He couldn't have hidden the pictures.
He circled and focused and framed. The breast and knee.
The purest art he said is the briefest art.

Once he hunted for love. A long time
he stood beside a little fat lady,
dressed in red, standing on the corner,
looking something like a fire hydrant.
She boarded a bus and left him there alone.

Daily the desperate ordering of this world,
the objects on his desk, the chosen words,
the knife, fork and spoon, the folded napkin,
the one, two, three, the counting, counting,
a constant laying of sandbags on the levee.

This poem's three scenes, like its title, make it gently mocking. "Once"—note—"he went inside a pool hall," but reminded by clicking balls of the African tribes who speak in clicks, the character retreats in awe from the shadowy figures skirting "the circles of light in a secret frenzy." He snaps away in life class, "breast and knee," without film in his Instamatic because "He couldn't have hidden the pictures." An unlikely "little fat lady, / dressed in red, standing on the corner," whom he stood beside mutely thinking of love, "boarded a bus and left him there alone." So, for him, the little things he can do, like knife, fork, and spoon, are "a constant laying of sandbags on the levee." They keep out the disorder at the edge of order that threatens to flood in.

Although the portrait is a caricature, the situation—the intimations of disorder or, what is the same thing, of *other* orders that threaten the limited order of ordinary life—is a paradigm in the poems of Miller Williams. Those threatened, notice, are not the blindly unquestioning or foolishly certain, but those open to possibilities, to imaginative awareness. Without doubt there can be no faith. A merely timid soul might realistically fear the rougher sorts who hang out in a pool hall, but the fellow in the poem sees them as tribal figures and responds to an alien order that they unknowingly represent.

As the poems that give "The Well-Ordered Life" its context in *Living on the Surface* make clear, the threat isn't the ultimate calamities themselves—which take no hostages, so to speak—but only intimations or resonances of them. In the poem before, "The Survivor," a reporter tries to interview the woman who alone survives a plane crash in the mountains. Just as she starts to answer, however, "the stretcher slipping," she plunges to her own death. The event itself is impenetrable. The poem turns to, and rebukes, the easy effort to find meaning:

> Some would say the ribbon she has in her hair
> fluttered loose when she fell and was found
> almost at once
> by a large bird, white, or more gray than white.
> This is not so.

In the poem that follows, an exploratory fantasy called "Getting the Message," Hermes—"looking like an ad for FTD"—appears to the speaker "here in a Houston hotel." The god's message, "in a swirling cursive, read / *What ought to happen happens in one year.*" The speaker, empowered by his promise not to reveal the message, declines to permit "what ought to happen" by (in the poem itself) revealing it. He concludes:

> Whatever it saved us from, or what it cost,
> whether I lost us heaven, or spared us hell,
> a die's uncast, a Rubicon uncrossed.

Balancing the risk of gain, the risk of loss, he opts for preserving the present, if limited and ambiguous, order of ordinary life. He will not, in Melville's phrase, strike through the mask.

The poems of Miller Williams often occur along this epistemological fault line between known order and perceived disorder, where intimations of the latter impinge. The impingements are frequently occasion for the poems, and the poems themselves such resolution of the tension as is possible. What is most noticeable over the years and books is the increasing subtlety, and the increasing humor, of the wisdom or resilience with which the balance is struck.

I propose to discuss this theme, the disorder on the edge of order, mostly in poems *not* included in Williams's most recent volume, *Living on the Surface*. I arrived at this odd way of proceeding by noticing the omission from the manuscript of two of my favorites; I resolved to sneak them back into print by quoting them . . . and it has been easy to opt for rescuing yet other poems.

1

Start with the sonnet "Politics" (from *Imperfect Love*):

> Mowing the lawn, having done with a tangle
> of briar, with yellow jackets in the eaves,
> he is imposing order, but he leaves
> some ragged grass where fences make an angle,
> trapping a small shadow most of the day.
> There, in the swarming morning, circling twice,
> his dog turns herself intently clockwise
> then drops on the flattened grass. In this way
> she reshapes the world to suit a hound.
> A square yard of his yard he leaves to her
> because he sees that both of them are bound
> as Jesus, Jefferson, and Caesar were
> (as all people are, and some small friends)
> to change a stubborn world to fit their ends.

The tone is benign. The man "is imposing order" on his part of "a stubborn world" and, perceiving the simultaneous otherness of his hound, leaves the grassy fence corner to her quite different ordering. In this, because she is a "small friend," he is politic. He sees that, "as all people are," "both of them are bound / as Jesus, Jefferson, and Caesar were" to the same effort of personally purposeful ordering. The descending rank of peaceableness implied in "Jesus, Jefferson, and Caesar" makes clear that politics—and every transaction is by nature political—may be a good deal less agreeable than in this case (man and his dog). The poem shields out the darker force of this realization (there can be no point in spoiling the pleasant summer day) but is aware of it (even if the man is not) in the fact of his "having done with a tangle / of briar, with yellow jackets in the eaves." The presence of that third order, momentarily dispersed, qualifies without denying the agreeable surface of this postlapsarian place and moment.

Williams's balancing in "Politics" is exquisite. We feel, as we read and ponder, more enriched than endangered by the awareness of disorder. Similarly, in the playful "Why I Go to Roger's Pool Hall" (*Why God Permits Evil*), bafflement seems enlarging and attractive:

> Pitcher I talked to told me he doesn't much like
> to strike a man out if he's barely hanging on.
> Every time I send him back to the benches
> I help make up the manager's mind to cut him.
> You think he thinks that every time he connects
> he drops my chances of getting called to Atlanta?
> Well I said I don't know. I never played baseball.

The infinitely interlocking circles of pitcher's and batter's awareness (or of the pitcher's awareness and speculation as to the batter's awareness) are logically amusing. The dilemma, we know, always resolves itself somehow in fact. There is no indication that either pitcher or batter acts, or could act, on the mutually connecting empathy. However in a given case it may turn out—batter "cut," pitcher "called to Atlanta," or most likely neither—we share the speaker's fascination with the apparently competing orders. It isn't his problem to deal with—"Well I said I don't know. I never played baseball"—and we are wonderfully armored by the blithe non sequitur. Life at Roger's emphatically local pool hall is touched only peripherally by the mysteries of the great world.

In an early poem, "Funeral" (*A Circle of Stone*), the character is more vulnerable to the alien order he chances upon.

> He pulled off on the shoulder, less to lend
> respect than room, because the road was narrow
> in the rain
> and saw the train creep painfully down the pavement
> past the bend
> to where his careful eyes had caught the sign
> of the Zion African Methodist Episcopal Church
> and an unpronounceable county line.
>
> Three faced three tall men straight and brown
> braced against its weight and let it down.

> He heard the shovel crunch and the dirt slip
> like a pump out of grease or an old man with asthma
> and though that preachers sin and doctors die
> was not even now a thing he would have thought of
> he turned to miss a rabbit caught in the lights
> and tried a while to say the name of the county
> before he found his speed and checked his watch
> and tuned in Memphis for the lightweight fights.

The vivid details of lowered coffin and shovel and dirt are of course his imagination of the scene: the procession he stops to let pass goes on "past the bend" to the churchyard he has already passed. Mortal ourselves, we understand the repression conveyed by the lack of a reference for the pronoun "it" that appears twice in the tenth line, as the troubling visualization intrudes. The compelled empathy of his turning "to miss a rabbit caught in the lights" and trying "a while to say the name of the county" finally dissipates as "he found his speed . . . / and tuned in Memphis for the lightweight fights." For a bit, however, the vision disrupts the comfortable progress of his own journey.

The strangeness of the experience depends in part on "his careful eyes," his having noted church and county line, much as the strangeness in the pool hall in "The Well-Ordered Life" depends on knowing about the African clicking language. The "unpronounceable" name of the county and his later trying to pronounce it symbolize the alien moment and his inability to reconcile it in his own life. If, as I think we do, we recall line 10's "weight" in the last line's contrasting "lightweight fights" in which other men face each other, the poem locks in—as with the yellow jackets in "Politics"—an uneasy awareness that transcends the driver's recovery of the ordinary.

In a number of poems the sheer multiplicity of potentially intersecting orders becomes the focus. The dizzying arithmetic of "After a Brubeck Concert," for instance:

> Six hundred years ago, more or less,
> something more than eight million couples
> coupled to have me here at last, at last.

Inverting the calculation, the speaker figures to have had after six hundred years the tiniest part in creating

> one
> barely imaginable, who may then be doing

something no one I know has ever done
or thought of doing, on some distant world
we did not know about when we were here.

"Or"—the poem ends in irony—"maybe sitting in a room like this, /
eating a cheese sandwich and drinking beer / . . . while two dogs, one
far away, answer bark for bark." The merely ordinary, in such a view,
looms as the strange and alien.

"Think Also of Horseshoes" (*So Long at the Fair*) traces, in a ritual of
instructions, the endless loopings-back of complexity in everyday reality:

Look at the nails on the wall
study the straight line
think of the man who hammered them years ago
he was a delta buck with a fat wife

Look at the tailgate bang on the back of a truck
think about the man who put it there
think of his daughter failing the fifth grade

Unwrap a cigar
think of the man who planted the tobacco
think of his dog peeing on the plants

Turn a rusty bottle cap out of the ground
think of the boy who drank the strawberry soda
think of him delivering The Democrat
chased by the dog run over
today by the truck
made by the man lost in Michigan
whose daughter is misspelling words for a Jew teacher
who writes *True Confessions* for the fat wife
of the diligent carpenter who is dead now.

Like the omniscient narrative voice of the more recent fantasy "One
Day a Woman," the voice here knows what we ordinarily do not. The
point seems to me less the actual coincidences recorded than the inevitable presence of such connections behind the usual two-dimension-
ality of experience. The title may remind us that a kingdom can be lost
for lack of a nail.

A waggish poem, "God" (*Distractions*), implies that the nearly infinite multiplicity defeats any knowledge:

If it weren't for the dog, I think it would be all right.
Not that it doesn't get old. It does get old.

> Try to keep in mind at the same time
> the constant green sedan that circles the block,
> the quadriplegic tied to the wheelchair,
> the head floating on nothing, the faith healer
> calling his dry mother, forth, come forth,
> yellow flowers on the windowsill,
> the president bringing the liquor to his lips,
> bending his head to help, his eyes aiming,
> the boy and the woman all a Saturday morning,
> twisting in the damp and happy sheets.
> Call them by name, call each of them a name.
> Love them, prepare to punish and love them all.
> Does anybody know whose dog that is?

Even God tires of trying "to keep in mind at the same time" all the variety, from green sedan circling the block to flowers on the sill or boy and woman making love. It's all too much, and even God loses track. "Does anybody know whose dog that is?"

2

For the individual, memory may provide disordering personal images of both multiplicity and simultaneity. The past may disconcert by becoming vividly present in the here and now, and identity seem dependent on the linking of disparate, competing scenes or experiences. Memory works just the way endless reruns do for the speaker in "The Aging Actress Sees Herself a Starlet on the Late Show":

> How would you like someone who used to be you
> fifty years ago coming into this room?
> How would you like it, never being able
> to grow old all together, to have yourself
> from different times of your life, running around?
>
> How would you like never being able
> to stop moving, always to be somewhere
> walking, crying, kissing, slamming a door?

We see from the outside an extreme of such disorientation in "Going" (*The Boys on Their Bony Mules*):

> The afternoon in my brother's backyard
> when my mother in awful age and failing
> in body not at all and twice the pity
> thought I was my dead father home for dinner

I didn't know what to tell her. What could I say?
Here I am home Darling give me your hand?
Let us walk together a little while?
Here it is 1915, we are married,
the first of our children is not yet born or buried,
the war in Europe is not yet out of hand
and the one you will not forget who wanted you first
is just as we are, neither old nor dead.
He still frets about us being together.

Good woman wife with five good children to mourn for,
and children arriving with children, what can I say?

See we have come because we wanted to come.
Because of love. Because of bad dreams.
This is my wife. We live in another state.

For the mother, a situation from the past has fixed itself upon the present; she sees her visiting son as her dead husband "home for dinner." An invasive past overwhelms the present. In responding, the speaker falls back, in the last lines, upon as much truth as can be mustered. The poem's varied and hitherto almost unnoticeable blank verse focuses in blunt, short sentences—the final line is metrically the clearest in the poem.

His hopeless imagination of what she perhaps expects as response fills eight lines (6–13). He fixes on what might seem the likeliest moment of her self-rewarding fantasy, the year of her marriage and presumably greatest happiness, before the calamity of the death of a first child and before the wider calamity of World War I has impinged (in whatever way) on the young couple. At the center of the projection, however, is the recollection of "the one you will not forget who wanted you first." The happiness, we see, is somehow fixed on this old infidelity, the illusion at least (if not the reality) of how she was loved by the rejected suitor. Painfully, what she mourns for, what she seems to long to recall, is no more than vanity or some dubious power derived from the jealousy of that long-vanished triangle—or even merely the shadow of another possible life that she did not choose. In imagining the father's response, the son speaks in the voice of the victim of her not forgetting "the one . . . who wanted you first," and that unhappiness, mirrored in the son, undercuts the mother's wish to live in a lost moment. We have come, he says, "Because of love. Because of bad dreams." Ambiguously, the title "Going" refers both to a time and world that are passing or passed and to the mother's mind in its dissociation. It also reverses the speaker's "See we have come" with his necessary distancing of himself from the mother's fantasy.

"A Game of Marbles" (*Why God Permits Evil*) shows the double vision memory can conjure up:

> Back in the town I used to live in
> I see some boys shooting marbles
> in the same empty lot.
>
> One of them shifting on his haunches
> looks up and sees me.

The implication is that the speaker sees, in the present boy "shifting on his haunches," a version of himself as he was some years ago. That the boy "looks up and sees me" completes the circuit, suggesting that without quite understanding, the boy, too, senses a strangeness in the man. The poem, however, states only the simple fact of the episode, in language so simple as to seem artless. But the doubling occurs silently in the syntax, in the repetition of *in* in the first line—"Back *in* the town I used to live *in*"—and perhaps in the way "same" in line 3 echoes "some" in line 2. The two stanzas, the larger one above, perhaps also mirror the scene, as do the parallel "I see" and he "sees," linking the man and boy in action. Two key words for their resonance in the poem's theme are "same" and "shifting." The man, containing the boy he was, both is and is not the same; measured by the spatial fixity of the empty lot, the image we have of him is as shifting as the boy, physically, is shifting on his haunches. The title, though it may be taken as plain notation, also seems resonant. We understand that the first sentence is completed by a suppressed clause like "in the same empty lot" where I as a boy was shooting marbles. That syntactical suppression nicely images the other, now vanished game of marbles. Or the two may be, in the title's singular, merely one archetypal game played in the "same" lot by the same boys timelessly.

A much more complex instance of the surprise of memory occurs in the elusive "He Notices One Morning How She Has Changed Again As It Were Overnight" (*Why God Permits Evil*). Memory and identity seem to separate, as the speaker conflates his experiences with three women, probably wives.

> That's twice.
>
> Where do you people come from?

Where do you go?
Conversations get cut off in the middle.
Hello. Already I miss her.
The way you get out of bed though.

They won't ever come back even at night.

Who wants them to.
They were good women. Let them go.

Someday you and I may think at the same time
of a restaurant in San Francisco or Tucson
and they will run into one another there
and not be surprised.

The speaker wakes, an apparently unexpected woman in bed with him. This is the second such occurrence ("That's twice"). He is baffled. "Where do you people come from? / Where do you go?"

The title suggests that it is a single woman—"she"—who has somehow "changed again as it were overnight," but we infer readily that "she" is a succession of women, each filling the same position in his life. The present one, to whom he addresses the questions and comment in lines 2–4 and the "Hello" in line 5, is the third; she is the "you" in line 6: "The way you get out of bed though." The second woman, displaced by this one, is the "her" in line 5: "Already I miss her." And the second woman, along with the first woman (whom the second obviously displaced in the same manner), are the "they" in lines 7 and 9. With a sense of sudden disorder, he waffles between missing the first two and the attractiveness of the third ("The way you get out of bed though") but by line 9 seems reconciled to the change, albeit without a diminished sense of the first two: "They were good women. Let them go." "Who wants them to [come back]" isn't a question, but an acceptance. The regretful recognition, emphasized by the one-line stanza, is that he has no choice: "They won't ever come back even at night." However the relationships in fact ended—in ways usual to marriage or whatever—the endings, he knows, are final. The women perhaps have the choice, but will not return; we may also gather that they left him. A clearly related poem is "A Good Woman," in the next book, *Distractions*, which describes such an ending:

But then it came to pass:
"Well," she said.
"Well," he answered. "Well. Alas. Alack."

> She kissed him on the head and shook his hand.
> "All's well that ends," she said, and never came back.
>
> You have to think of Eve . . .

All this has a fine comic poignancy. "He Notices One Morning How She Has Changed Again As It Were Overnight"—need it be said—is amusing and in some measure satiric. Only very generally, however, is the point of the satire the musical beds or musical marriages (so to speak) of recent decades, or even the speaker's exaggerated passivity or refusal of responsibility. For him, it is all a rather magical experience. The poem, it seems to me, is meant to embody a genuine disorientation—like déjà vu—in the appearance of persistence in the identity of the "woman" he believes embodied in all three wives or lovers. Sharing his life with each, he has the illusion that somehow they must therefore equally share that common experience.

Hence, the last stanza. The projection is fragile—only "Someday" and "may" in line 10—and depends upon the speaker and the third woman thinking "at the same time" of the restaurant.

> Someday you and I may think at the same time
> of a restaurant in San Francisco or Tucson
> and they will run into one another there
> and not be surprised.

Little is obvious about this magical thinking. Presumably, although San Francisco or Tucson could be any city, there is some relevance in these particular cities. They must be cities where he knows a restaurant and where, we may guess, he took one or the other (or separately both) of the first two women. It seems to be a condition that he and the third woman think of the restaurant independently, by chance or perhaps out of nostalgia. One leap in his thinking is that the third woman would know a restaurant in either place, to which he had gone with one or both of the others. A second leap is that the first two women would, therefore, appear at that restaurant and so run into and recognize one another. A third leap is that they would "not be surprised" at this occurrence. The only thing that can justify these leaps is that the three women in fact share a single identity. Only in the title, which uses the third person, is that assumption explicit. In the poem proper, when he speaks, they are distinct—though he puzzles over their apparently causeless succession.

We don't know what real circumstances are concealed by this

account. But beneath them—I think the poem argues—beneath the causes and effects, the reasons and the conclusions, there is an emotional level that is very close to fantasy. It may break through only momentarily, as in the speaker's rudimentary sense of things in the transition of awakening. The poem's poignancy comes in part from our seeing, from the vantage point of everyday common sense, how fragile is his hope of restoring, somehow, in the first two women's meeting at whatever indefinite future time, the whole circuit of his feeling and experience.

3

The intrusion of an unsettling order in the guise of fantasy appears in several poems in Williams's first collection, *A Circle of Stone*, notably in "Depot in a River Town" and "For Robert, *Son of Man*," in which a five-year-old boy's discovery of his sexuality appears to his father to involve them in age-old ritual, as of some Stonehenge. Howard Nemerov has noted the pun sun/son.

> and we are together
> in a circle of stone
> where the sun slips red and new
> to a stand of oak.

In "Depot in a River Town" the somnolent station is transformed for the speaker into the classical myth of Charon's ferry:

> In the depot and the darkened day
> the clack of an old pinball machine
> demands a curious notice.
> More sleeping than not
> a satchel faced farmer makes noises.
> A sailor circles like a child in church.
>
> In the depot and the darkened day
> I surrender my back to the imperative bench,
> unlistening hear the emphatic pencil
> tap itself on the table.
>
> The little blonde reads
> and fingers the cloth of her blouse
> like a nun telling beads.
>
> Cracked across after an ancient painting
> the face of the woman with children
> ignores and ignores.

There is fog at the windows
and the open doors.

Within the ear's rim rises a separate sound.
Wood slapping side slipping water sounds
settle me deep.
I feel again the penny in my pocket
and the slow sleep of the river
wraps me round.

Details slowly accumulate an impression that, by the last stanza, turns into the drowsing speaker's sense that the awaited journey is across the river into Hades. Only the pinball machine belongs to the twentieth century, and it is "old." The slightly archaic words "depot" and "satchel" (as image for the farmer's face), along with the also metaphorical "ancient painting," lend an illusion of the past; and the similes "like a child in church" and "like a nun telling beads" add a sense of religious occasion. The general desultoriness of the scene is crossed by a series of unexpected forceful words—"demands," "imperative," "emphatic," and perhaps "Cracked across." Just as we don't at first particularly notice the sailor, we aren't aware of whose pencil might "tap itself on the table" or why with emphasis, nor at first of what (the syntax remains incomplete) the woman "ignores and ignores." The "fog at the windows / and the open doors" recalls the presence of the river at the crucial moment and suggests a timeless and muffled landscape.

The first noticeable rhyme occurs in stanza 3, "reads-beads," though we may have unlistening heard "notice-noises" in stanza 1, or "day-table" and "bench-pencil" in stanza 2. Only with "ignores-doors" in stanza 4 is it certain that the rhyme in stanza 3 is not by chance. The last stanza's increment—"sound-sounds-round" and the twisting external and internal "deep-sleep"—images the circling in toward fatal sleep. There is, too, "slap-slip-sleep-wraps" and a density of alliteration echoing that of "In the depot and the darkened day," which had seemed hitherto ominous only by chance. The fantasy is carefully orchestrated, but ambiguously. It may be taken as merely the dozing-off impression of a rather literary speaker in a generally gloomy but not really threatening scene. The disorder is in the speaker's own perception.

In a number of later poems Williams works out similarly disquieting intuitions or symbols in overt, often comic fantasies of violence. "Love and How It Becomes Important in Our Day to Day Lives," for instance, satirizes the invasive intimacy of television commercials; in the last stanza we are almost invited to interpret the speaker as nearly asleep and dreaming before the TV:

> Then comes my wife as if to wake me up,
> a box of ammunition in her arms.
> She settles herself against the wall beside me.
> "The towns are gone," she says. "They're taking the farms."

"Late Show," in its final stanza when the character in the story on TV addresses the transfixed viewer ("Turn it off, he says, in god's name"), explores a viewer's complicity in the fictions he or she watches. If it seems that the man with the gun is entering the viewer's room ("The door opens. A man with a long gun. / He takes aim"), the fantasy remains as ambiguous as Charon's ferry is in "Depot in a River Town." And the wonderful poem "I Go Out of the House for the First Time" symbolically translates the effect of guilt or shame into disturbing narrative.

"About the Airplane, Then" (*Distractions*) amusingly projects the interlocking of perception and understanding:

> Looking out the window, across the room,
> I saw a plane heading toward the west.
> I thought as I often do when I see a plane
> of who might be on board and what they wish
> they'd said before they left or not said,
> those they love and those they meant to love.
> The plane seemed so small at such a distance,
> and seemed to move so slowly, it might have been
> some little creature crawling across the screen.
> It stopped as if to consider that a while,
> changed directions slightly and crawled on.
>
> Inside my head two hundred and seventy people
> including a crew of eleven disappeared
> leaving no trace but only vacancies
> at typewriters, bedtime and breakfast. It came so fast
> nobody had a hint of what was coming
> except for one especially perceptive
> flight attendant who seemed to be startled
> about something just at the last moment.

The first stanza in effect offers two interpretations of the plane watched in its slow passage by the speaker. The first, in lines 2–6, is a rather sentimental projection of human concerns that might be dramatized in the journeys of the passengers. The second, in lines 7–11, seems more trustworthy. It reports what he sees. But what he sees, reduced by distance, is hardly true to the fact. And the image of "some little creature crawling across the screen" and seeming to pause as if in thought is of course far more interpretative or manipulative than the sentimental one. Either way, the plane exists essentially in his awareness of it.

When he turns his attention away, it will disappear, "leaving no trace." The conceit of the vanishing of "two hundred and seventy people / including a crew of eleven" occurs, he knows, only "inside my head." But the completion of the imagined event is inevitable, and the one "especially perceptive / flight attendant," from inside the fantasy, seems to mirror his awareness, "startled / about something just at the last moment." Epistemologically, the poem ends in a draw. The troubling disorder is not *out there,* but *in here,* inside the perception, as in the daring and playful "One Day a Woman," in which the drawings up into the air of a woman in Georgia and a man in Kansas are attested to as facts beyond doubt. "The children were disbelieved" as to the first, the usual knowledge being accepted as sufficient; but "the dozen well-known / and highly respected citizens" who witnessed the second could not be doubted.

> Nobody who knew about the first event
> knew of the second, so no connection was made.
> The tarbrush fell to earth somewhere in Missouri
> unnoticed among a herd of Guernsey cows.

Comic piquancy comes from our realizing that we know, and so are able to make the connection, only through the narrator's voice. But what, then, can "Nobody" mean? And what, we may wonder, must we make of the word "unnoticed" in the last line?

Here, like the speaker in "About the Airplane, Then," we suddenly find ourselves standing just a little beyond the edge of a precipice. As Williams puts it in the poem from *The Boys on Their Bony Mules* that gives title and theme to *Living on the Surface,*

> Jesus, we've only just got here.
> We try to do what's right
> but what do we know?

 *Just a Good Read*

William Stafford

Miller Williams is one of those writers whose books drag me snorkeling happily along. Happy as a pig among truffles, I hurry to the next treasure.

Sniffing at other books sometimes I hark back to when I was considering a whole range of readings in a contest and came upon Miller's *Why God Permits Evil*—immediately I switched from duty reading to headlong, though sometimes horrified, pursuit. What's going on? Where is this guy taking me? What is this mixture of hillbilly voice and jagged insights in a pitiless light?

Well, some distinctions account for my addiction to such books. They go along in the main stream of talk, carrying plenty of freight and seeming to be direct as an arrow that departs for an objective with no interference from convention or ordinary timidities in language. There are frequent verbal events, surprises, quirks. It is all like talk with luck in it, and that's my usual way of identifying my preference in literature.

But there is more. Miller's poems evidence serious concerns related to ordinary people, but with a constant elevation that comes from irony and control. There are abrupt drops into brutal directness from elevated language. Even when the lines are full of pity and fear, they are funny, with abundant expectation and release from the expected. Powerful, common cliché-beliefs recur, tinged with irony but retaining their hold on our imaginations: Miller can't leave religion out; he uses the grooves of popular belief and gives them his own kind of curving, bent-over concern. He can't leave our central fears and guilts alone, but they come into the poems in a setting of unstoppable appetite for life. The total vision is grim, but illuminated by the vigor of the seeing.

Amid my spells of admiration I have to pause for deep, troubling questions of my own: Does good writing have to confront the gravity of first and last things that we slight and go around and suppress in our daily living? Is it right, is it just, is it fair to hold us fallible beings so firmly in place before undeniable grim truths? Our lives have those truths in them, but mostly they float more serenely, buoyant for their very weaknesses, their charming, warm, forgivable happiness.

Shouldn't a literature that is true to the feel of our lives have a preponderance of hope over despair? Books that dwell on sadness are not, most of the time, true. Maybe?

But then I am back in the Miller Williams book, being excited and stirred, finding the voice of someone who cares so much that what blights a life must be faced down with clarity, irony, humor, tenacity. I find poems like "Style" that delight me and make me vibrate with sympathy. Or poems like "The Senator Explains a Vote," with its level voice to say: "One of the hardest things we have to do / is face the awful fact of the ordinary." (But this is the voice of the senator—is it Miller's voice?)

Then there is "The Promotion," a dramatic monologue to match "My Last Duchess." And even the titles to give a shiver and make into strange mixtures—"The Voice of America," "The Only World There Is."

And there is "Let Me Tell You"; it is about how to be a writer. Miller Williams is scary. He knows too much.

II.

A POEM FOR EMILY

✓ We are set apart — I am fifty three —
by two generations, which is the way
— considering what's between us — it ought to be.
You are not yet a full day.

✓ When I am sixty three and you are ten
and you have known me since the world began
perhaps you'll teach me what you've learned by then
and ask me what I'll tell you if I can.

When I am eighty nine years old, and you
are thirty six and have a family
you built yourself including one or two
children who look nothing at all like me,

~~notice with ~~ ~~how you will have read them this~~
✓ one time I know you will have read them this
so they will know I love them and tell them so
and love their mother. Child, whatever is,
is always or never was. ~~Long though ago,~~ Long ago,

✓ a day I watched a while beside your bed,
I wrote this down, ~~something~~ that might be kept
a ~~short~~ while to say ~~what~~ something I would have said
when you were who knows what and I was dead
which is I stood and loved you while you slept.

 *The Poetry*

Form and Informality

X. J. Kennedy

Readers who have closely followed Miller Williams's career as a poet, and those who know his critical guidebook *Patterns of Poetry* (1986), know that for Williams traditional forms have long held a powerful fascination. All through the *Howl*-dominated Dark Ages in American poetry, he persisted in his fondness for meter and rhyme, falling into their fruitful restraints whenever a poem called for them. As his 1986 collection *Imperfect Love* shows, and his newer work besides, several of the best of his recent poems are cast in traditional forms or in variants of them. In these remarks, I would like to guess what meter and rhyme have meant to Williams, and point with admiration to some of the ways he has used them to large effect.

Admittedly, I will be looking at Williams's work with blinders on. To speak only of those poems written in rhyme and meter is, of course, to speak only of part of his poetry. Obviously, much of his finest work is in free or open verse, which discovers its own laws as it goes along. But I want to consider a few clear-cut illustrations of those poems written in consistent rhyme schemes, other poems in which rhyme seems central and indispensable, and several other interesting poems in traditional fixed forms. I will dwell mainly on the text of *Living on the Surface: New and Selected Poems*, the poet's own choice of work on which he stands ready to be judged.

Even when venturing into open form, Williams appears to retain a sense of tradition. Meter, it would seem, keeps echoing in his inner ear, as the words of a fundamentalist preacher might still nag a man who has quit the church. Often a poem that at first glance looks freewheeling and unregulated will prove, on closer inspection, to be iambic in its measures. Sometimes a passage when scanned will reveal such regularity, and its thoughts will turn on rhymes.

43

> With hands that could have torn the hills apart
> the preacher hammered the tinfoil of my faith
> and words came teaching me
> out of the terrible whirlwind of his mouth
> the taste of evil
> bitter and hot as belch
> the agony of God
> building the gospel word by believable word
> out of the wooden syllables of the South

This from "And When in Scenes of Glory," an early poem. The off-rhymes *faith* and *mouth, evil* and *belch, God* and *word,* suggest—but do not compel—a tight structure of argument.

In his refusal to commit himself totally to strict meter while maintaining a lifelong fondness for it, Williams reminds me of his friend John Ciardi, a devotee of strait form who never (except in his children's verse) restricted himself exclusively to it. A browse through *Living on the Surface* shows that Williams has preserved traditionally formal poems from every one of his previous eight collections. Among the new poems, nine out of fifteen are clearly formal. I mention these figures only to suggest that for Williams strict form is no passing fancy.

Like any competent rhyming poet who has written a great deal, Williams at his best does not bend rhymes to his thought, but thinks in rhyme. In his first book, *A Circle of Stone,* in "The Associate Professor Delivers an Exhortation to His Failing Students," the rhyming words draw closer and closer together as the professor warms to his exhortation.

> tell them failing is an act of love
> because
> like sin
> it is the commonality within

Another poem from that first collection, "Original Sin," is cast wholly in a demanding rhymed stanza. The speaker recalls what seems his adolescent loss of virginity to a movie-house ticket-seller.

> In bed my hand
> was cold still and the fingers I let pretend
> that she was lying
> white on a blue hill,
> birds flying.

Seeming unforced, these rhymes fall on ordinary words. To this day,

Williams generally prefers to rhyme words that do not call attention to themselves. Among the new poems, "For Reuben, at Twelve Months" exhibits the power that strict form can give to language deliberately simple and (for the most part) ordinary.

> Whatever else you come to be
> you will always be a year,
> with numbers starting out from here
> and going past where I can see,
> if you are clever and cock an ear
> for beast of old and boast of new,
> if you are careful and keep an eye
> peeled for the trolls of derring-do.
> It took some luck to come this far.
> That's half the game, to see how high
> a number you can say you are.

Addressed to the child, mostly in words of one syllable, the poem begins casually, almost flatly, then commences playing with words (*beast* and *boast*). With the introduction of trolls, it enters the universe of fairy tales. Had it been cast in free verse, this winning poem could have seemed banal, despite its playfulness. High-handedly written to remove its rhyme and mess up its meter, it might have read:

> Whatever else you may be
> you will always be a year,
> with numbers starting out
> and going past my line of sight,
> if you are clever and listen
> for beast of old and boast of new,
> and keep an eye peeled
> for the derring-do trolls.
> It took some luck for you to come all this way.
> That's half the game, to see how high
> a number you reach.

Those crude lines, obviously not by Miller Williams, should be enough to indicate his art. With dexterity, Williams couples informal language to strait form, as did Robert Frost, another poet under whose sway Williams, a sometime resident at the Bread Loaf Writers Conference, no doubt came. Frost early insisted on the value of breaking colloquial phrases across the steel of a metrical beat, taking advantage of what he called "the sound of sense."

Williams has proved himself a master of the most demanding, and sustaining, of all forms, those elaborate ones that come down to us from French courtly poetry. "On the Way Home from Nowhere, New Year's Eve," from *Why God Permits Evil*, not only fulfills the intricate pattern of the sestina, but with great skill relates a dramatic incident. Pausing late at night at his office in a campus building, the speaker finds the lights turned off, and he suddenly feels himself one with his thirteen-year-old self, stricken by a terror of the dark. The poem becomes a meditation on form; indeed, *form* is one of the six words repeated in its pattern. The dull, uncertain formlessness of things glimpsed in the dark heightens the speaker's fear: darkness is full of supernatural beings, "old mythologies of daytime and the dark / spun by gods and monster movies." The occasion—New Year's Eve—reminds the speaker that time is passing; and time, with its power to dissolve and destroy, is form without space.

> Going on, I grab some papers off
> some desk in the dark and turn back toward the light
> I barely remember, running, hungry for form.

Form and sense here combine memorably. A more recent sestina, "Love in the Cathedral," from *Imperfect Love*, distributes its syntax freely and naturally and speakably throughout this strict traditional form; I would quote, but the poem needs to be read and savored entire:

LOVE IN THE CATHEDRAL
"... except you ravish me."

> In the beginning I couldn't speak to you.
> Not because the words wouldn't come;
> it was because they might. Not words like love,
> blooming where they fall; words like come here.
> When once you turned to look straight at me
> out of a crowd, I thought I must have let
>
> the sounds inside my head come out, like "let
> us all go home." I wouldn't say to you
> the wet, small words that moved inside of me.
> I have thought that faith and patience would come
> to no good end, that you would say, "See here!"
> and never say, "Well yes, I think I'd love
>
> to follow you home; to tell the truth, I'd love
> to have some wine, then talk awhile, then let

you pleasure me." *Expelled to suffer here,*
John Milton wrote of us. I look at you
and in my mind your awful kinsmen come
around every corner, looking for me.

You once talked about the weather with me
and that was something, but it was not love,
did not resemble love. Love ought to come
in recognizable clothes. One day I let
my plain and earthy self talk to you
most gently, saying plainly, "Please come here,"

but everything went wrong, a bah-bah here,
a bah-bah there. You have bumped into me
by accident, I have bumped into you
on purpose on the street where talk of love
was inappropriate, then I have let
my heart hide in the cold and watched you come

laughing and blind. No matter what may come,
give me this: that all this time I stood here
ignored to death and loved you while you let
every chance go; say your glances at me
suggested almost anything but love;
say I know you cry in bed, poor you.

Believe in love. You know that I am here
to let you loose. Here is my flesh for you
who may abide with me till kingdom come.

Like the sestina, the form of the villanelle lends more support (and imposes more restrictions) than most experienced poets want; it is a favorite form of novices who wish sustaining. As soon as one writes the lines to be repeated, the poem is almost half done, but the difficult trick is to make its insistent repetitions seem to occur naturally. *Living on the Surface* preserves a single masterly specimen, "For Lucinda, Robert, and Karyn," also from the late book *Imperfect Love*. In it, the poet appears to set forth, in speakable language, a last will and testament. It seems to me one of the best villanelles in English; I know of few better.

I leave you these, good daughters and honest son,
to have or toss away
when all is said and done:

a name that rocks like a boat; some thoughts begun;
a fondness for instruments I didn't play.
I leave you these, fair daughters and far son:

a sense of the probable (the one
sure anchor for the brain); a place to stay
as long as it stands. When all is said and done

you'll share the glory I won, or might have won,
for things I said or things I meant to say.
I leave you these, tough daughters and rocky son:

a tick no springs or brain or batteries run;
a valley in the mattress where I lay.
When all is said and done,

I'll leave my unpaid debts to everyone,
a slow love and resentment's sweet decay.
I'll leave you to yourselves, my daughters, my son,
when what's to say and do has been said and done.

Ordinary speech is seldom so well managed in poetry. Even the cliché "when all is said and done" actually springs to life. Williams triumphs by riding roughshod over the villanelle's rules, and by adapting them to his purposes.

Except in translating the sonnets of Giuseppe Belli, Williams has ventured only occasionally into the sonnet form. "How Does a Mad-song Know That's What It Is?" (*Why God Permits Evil*) and the appealing "Jonathan Aging" (*Imperfect Love*) are perhaps his sonnets most clearly bound by conventional rules. Eliot said that often, in reading free verse, he heard the ghost of form lurking behind the arras; and the ghost of the sonnet seems to lurk in Williams's thirteen-line "Mecanic on Duty at All Times" (the misspelling is deliberate), a superb portrait of a family down on its luck.

The license plate was another state and year.
The man's slow hands, as if they had no part
in whatever happened here, followed the hollows
and hills of his broad belt. Inside the car
four children, his face again, with eyes like washers,
were as still as the woman, two fingers touching her cheek.
"How much?" he said. "Well maybe fifty dollars
if I can find a used one. I guess I can."
The hands paid no attention. Out in the sun
light wires rose and dipped and dipped again

until they disappeared. *Flats fixed* and *Gas*
and *Quaker State* squeaked in the wind. Just like that.
And the speeding trucks, wailing through their tires.

The rough rhymes *year* and *car, washers* and *dollars, can* and *sun* and
again suggest a poem struggling to be a sonnet, and deciding not to.
And the disorderly, incomplete realization of this scheme seems part of
the meaning: stasis, frustration, a sense of things broken down, incon-
clusiveness. This short poem seems to me among Williams's finest in
Imperfect Love, a strong collection.

A remarkable near-sonnet that rhymes only with assonance, "A News-
paper Picture of Spectators at a Hotel Fire" (*The Boys on Their Bony
Mules*) contains rhymes almost too far out to notice.

At three in the afternoon on a clear day
fire breaks out in a tall St. Louis hotel
on the 16th floor and takes it from end to end.

That is how high above this street of faces
as fixed as stones three women stood in windows
with cracking glass behind them till one by one
they tested the air like swimmers and stepped stiffly out.
They come down with zeroes in their mouths.

One among the watchers has turned his back
on such important people who step into nothing,
who kick their way to the curb, to the tops of cars.
He takes away what he wants, the negative faces.

All morning we are moody. We mention the picture,
the long, slow arms, the women falling toward us.

Again, the poem seems to aspire to sonnetdom, changes its mind, and
achieves something impressive on its own. The final image of terrible
suspense, of the slowly falling women, seems to me much more effective with its hint at rhyme than it would have been with a loudly chim-
ing one.

Those almost-sonnets, or whatever they are, are remarkable poems.
Still, it may be that Williams's most considerable gift to the history of
the sonnet in English is his *Sonnets of Giuseppi Belli.* This popular
poet of Rome, author of raunchy, irreverent, and anti-clerical sonnets
in the Romanesco dialect (or language), surely found in Miller Williams
his ideal translator. Two masters of slang and colloquial speech in

poetry, Belli and Williams recast familiar biblical tales in remarkably up-to-date speech.

> "But, Jesus Christ," said Martha, "I've had it to here
> with Mary Magdalene. I cannot take her
> rosaries, her novenas anymore.
> I open my mouth and she calls me a troublemaker.

The apparent ease of these translations—which must have cost Williams dear—seems phenomenal; the shrewdness and earthy humor of the original surmount the language barrier.

How venturesome has Williams been in his handling of other forms? One of the boldest and most successful of his experiments is "Rubaiyat for Sue Ellen Tucker," a folk-ballad story told in—of all things—the pseudo-Persian stanza favored by Edward FitzGerald. Despite this source, the language of the poem escapes all bookishness.

> She had the baby and then she went to the place
> She heard he might be at. She had the grace
> To whisper who she was before she blew
> The satisfied expression from his face.

"Ghosts," a meditation in quatrains, succeeds in a radical formal strategy: it rhymes by repeating words, so that words rhyme with themselves.

> Some evenings, there are ghosts. There are. Ghosts
> come in through the door when people come in,
> being unable to open doors themselves
> and not knowing (not knowing they are ghosts)
>
> they could pass through anything, like thought.
> They come and stand, move aimlessly about
> as if each one of them had come to meet
> someone who hadn't arrived. I always thought
>
> of haunts and spirits as having a special power
> like witches to do whatever they wanted to.
> They don't. Pure energy without a cage
> can do nothing at all. Whatever power
>
> pushes or pulls the things of this world
> to any purpose does it by piston or pistol,
> millwheel or spring or some such pushing back.
> Spirit freed fades into the world.

And on for another eight stanzas. Williams runs serious risks here: of boring readers, or encouraging them to guess in advance the closing line of each quatrain. But his gamble pays off, and we read on, compelled to follow a casual discussion of a subject immense and disquieting.

Like every form-loving poet, Williams knows that forms convey unexpected power when a poet chooses to shatter their rules. A poem whose language is mostly quiet and casual, "A Summer Afternoon an Old Man Gives Some Thought to the Central Questions" has a form so gently enforced that you hardly notice it. The poem begins with evident rhymes, then falls out of rhyme, as though deliberately.

> So it is at the end
> but who would want to be an old house
> who, being hammered on all day,
> understood nothing?

In the early "Voice of America" (*The Only World There Is*), Williams also sidesteps the rules. Written in quatrains, the poem builds force from its refrain, "Do not imagine . . . Do not imagine." It may be variously read, but I take it to be an official directive to a soldier who must kill in war, warning him, lest he feel compassion, against thinking of the tremendous preparations that went into his victim's conception, gestation, and birth. Formally, the poem boldly keeps to a strict rhyme scheme for three dozen lines, then inserts a jarring off-rhyme into the penultimate stanza, and into the last stanza a startling expanse of white space that compels a pause.

> Do not imagine the enormous eyes.
> Do not imagine the chin sits
> soft against the uncovered heart.
> Do not imagine the gill slits,
>
> the hands unfinished, the tail shrinking.
> Do not imagine the time at hand
> or what it means. Raise the gun.
> Hold it gently as you were trained
>
> to hold it. Let the bullet swim
> slowly into his opening head
> fast as sperm   the way the films
> in school can show a flower spread.

Formally inventive too, "Late Show," a narrative, is cast in tight quatrains whose fourth lines fall short.

> Too tired to sleep I switch a picture on,
> turn down the sound to let my attention drain.
> A forest in summer. Dogs. A man is running.
> It's starting to rain.

More usual, ballad-like quatrains accommodate "How the Elephant Got His Hump," a lighthearted mock fable that imagines the invention of the martini. Meant to be a poison, the mixture of gin and vermouth instead regales a king, its intended victim. Rare in the Williams canon, this lightweight, delectable item seems almost a takeoff on A. E. Housman's "Terence, This Is Stupid Stuff" and displays Williams's skill in adapting strait forms to light verse.

Because it's so brief, I can't resist citing, too, one more illustration of Williams's lighter side, "My Wife Reads the Paper at Breakfast on the Birthday of the Scottish Poet":

> Poet Burns to Be Honored, the headline read.
> She put it down. "They found you out," she said.

Remove the rhyming form and the basis in pentameter, and all that would remain would be a one-liner. As it stands, it's a flawless epigram.

Ordinarily, though, when Williams employs couplets he makes them tell a story, or advance some serious purpose. Perhaps his finest poem in couplets is the relatively long "Some Lines Finished Just Before Dawn at the Bedside of a Dying Student It Has Snowed All Night." It ends in language that could hardly be less ornate.

> The nurse will disturb you soon. I will say
> good morning again. I will mention the snow.
> I will lie about this. I will get my coat
> and tie my shoes. I will stop and stand
> by the bed a while and hold your hand
> longer than you like for me to
> and drive home dying more slowly than you.

To write in rhyme is to risk a failure that will be obvious. When rhyme works—as I think it does here—it clicks. It stamps its poem with a certain inevitable resonance. When it doesn't work it causes a poem to clunk painfully. Naturally, not all of Williams's rhymed poems seem to me equally successful; at times we can foresee a rhyme coming. In his choice of poems for *Living on the Surface*, Williams has dropped numbers of formal poems that didn't click. His taste has been sure, although I would have argued for the retention of "Remembering Walter" from *Halfway to Hoxie,* his earlier new-and-selected poems. Still, some of the new poems make up for such a loss. The reader who would check me out should read (in particular) "Thinking about Bill, Dead of Aids," "Before," "Missing Persons" (incidentally, a poem entirely in off-rhymes), "Rituals," "An August Evening Outside of Nashville," "He Speaks to His Arguing Friends and to Himself," and "A Glass Darkly"—this last memorable poem closing the book on a rhyme.

> The lady wiping up
> said, "Do you want another?" He said, "No'm,
> I better not." Still he didn't leave.
> "Where are you from," I said. He said, "Home."

In *Who's Who in America,* whose editors solicit sage advice from their biographees, Williams makes a revealing statement (unlike most such pronouncements, not the least bit pontifical): "The human mind has a rage for order. The sane mind seeks the order inherent in every event; the insane mind imposes an order of its own invention upon the events around it. This is the only distinction, so far as I know, that matters." If Williams's poems frequently see order in a disorderly world, they seem concerned no less to discover whatever order inheres in informal speech. Sanity, it seems, is a matter of controlling the language—or such is the point of "A Little Poem" from *Imperfect Love,* another triumph of speaking of deep matters casually and simply and clearly, within the demands of form.

> We say that some are mad. In fact
> if we have all the words and we
> make madness mean the way they act
> then they as all of us can see
>
> are surely mad. And then again
> if they have all the words and call
> madness something else, well then—
> well then, they are not mad at all.

Although traditional form has always mattered to Williams, in his late work it seems more central than ever. Reading him, I feel that a strict form is never—as many who misunderstand such forms expect—an empty box to be crammed with nondescript words. For Williams, meter and rhyme are instruments of feeling. Most contemporary poets might well go to him for lessons in the art of speaking plainly in disciplined lines alive with emotional energy.

 The Dramatic Monologues

John Frederick Nims

Living on the Surface, with over a dozen new poems added to its generous selection of work from eight earlier books, shows us what Miller Williams, as poet, has accomplished over the last twenty-five years. That he has managed to write so much while teaching, editing, translating, and sojourning abroad is something to marvel at; that he has done all this with ease and grace is something the world of literature can be grateful for.

His voice, I think we feel, has remained his own over the years. Robert Frost, in one of his earliest poems, said that if friends of his youth were to overtake him long afterward, "They would not find me changed from him they knew— / Only more sure of all I thought was true." This could just as well be said of Miller Williams. But though the voice is the same, the range of subjects it has found to deal with is a far-reaching one.

"Notes from the Agent on Earth: How to Be Human" presents some of the figures in the drama of his work: Love, Loneliness, Fear, Ambition, Faith, Will to Power, Envy, Covetousness, Death. In other poems there are still more that he leaves uncapitalized: science, religion, family, apparitions, mythology, travel (from America to Chile to India), and countless other topics ranging from the space-time continuum to the invention of the martini, things that make up "daily the desperate ordering of the world," both the realistic world of our senses and the world of eerie otherness.

In a number of poems a character, or the poet, soliloquizes on these and other topics; in recent years the soliloquies have broadened into dramatic monologues. Eight of these monologues are what I would like to focus on in this necessarily partial tribute to Williams's achievement.

In thinking of the dramatic monologue, we probably evoke first the name of its most eminent practitioner. In the collections he called *Dramatic Lyrics, Dramatic Romances and Lyrics, Dramatis Personae,* and

Dramatic Idyls, Robert Browning gave the monologue the form we are familiar with. Williams, who knows these poems well, might willingly make a bow in Browning's direction, as Dante does in Virgil's when he addresses him as "il mio maestro e 'l mio autore."

In a dramatic monologue, the poet assumes a persona who reveals something of his own soul as he talks to a listener or listeners; the setting and situation may suggest, as often in Browning, a dynamic relationship between the parties. In his best-known monologues, Browning likes to make the characters and situation clear in the first few lines, though our knowledge of both deepens in the course of the poem. In "My Last Duchess" the Duke sets the scene by indicating a portrait and saying, "Will't please you sit and look at her?" Later we learn that the "you" is an emissary, otherwise uncharacterized, from a Count whose daughter the Duke is scheming to marry. In "The Bishop Orders His Tomb at St. Praxed's Church" the scene is set more rapidly as the Bishop gathers his illegitimate sons (his "nephews") around him on his deathbed: "Draw round my bed: is Anselm keeping back? / Nephews—sons mine." In "Fra Lippo Lippi" the friar is stopped by the night watchmen making their rounds:

> I am poor brother Lippo, by your leave!
> You need not clap your torches to my face. . . .
> What, 'tis past midnight, and you go the rounds,
> And here you catch me at an alley's end
> Where sportive ladies leave their doors ajar?

"Andrea del Sarto" also opens with the stage set: the painter is appealing to his beautiful but indifferent wife and model, whose mind is on the impatient whistles of her "cousin" outside. She says nothing, but once or twice the poet gives us a clue to her reactions. The longer, less familiar monologues begin in the same way. Bishop Blougram opens his "Apology" with "No more wine? then we'll push back chairs and talk." *He* talks; his listener, "Gigadibs the literary man," whose frivolous name tells us something about him, apparently says nothing, but the Bishop imagines and rebuts his objections. "Mr. Sludge, 'The Medium,'" Bernard Shaw's favorite Browning poem, begins with physical violence, as Mr. Sludge (based on an American "medium" whom Browning thought a fraud and referred to as a "dung-ball") grovels before the enraged listener he tries to win over with blandishments.

> Now, don't, sir! Don't expose me! Just this once!
> This was the first and only time, I'll swear,—

> Look at me,—see, I kneel,—the only time,
> I swear, I ever cheated . . .
>   Aie—aie—aie!
> Please, sir! your thumbs are through my windpipe, sir!

In Williams's dramatic monologues, the titles themselves may identify speaker and listener, as in "The Ghost of His Wife Comes to Tell Him How It Is." In "Missing Persons" a subtitle explains that "A Neighbor Tells the Officer What He Knows," though—and this is unusual in a dramatic monologue—he says nothing about himself. In "The Senator Explains a Vote," setting and listeners are revealed in the first two lines:

> It's not my office, after all; it's yours.
> I'm always pleased to see the folks I work for.

In "*In Extremis* in Hardy, Arkansas" the first line and a half show us a lawyer in a courtroom addressing a jury. "The Promotion" has a businessman talking to dinner guests. "Ruby Tells All" has a waitress in a coffee shop talking to a customer, as is the moonshiner in "Rituals." "The Journalist Buys a Pig Farm" has the speaker talking to an unidentified somebody. In several of these, the identity and behavior of the listener are not reported.

Williams's monologues are all contemporary; one of their merits is the conviction of reality we get from a kind of speech we recognize as genuinely colloquial. They recall the use Frost made of the interplay between colloquial speech and formal meter—a kind of dynamic counterpoint in which Williams also excels. Though his diction, like Frost's, has the ring of reality, the poems of his we are considering are technically different from those of the older master. Frost's poems are not dramatic monologues so much as soliloquies in which he is talking to himself or to the world in general ("Mending Wall"), or third-person dramatic narratives with more than one speaker ("The Death of the Hired Man"). Perhaps the one dramatic monologue of his we can think of that is in the manner of Browning (and of Williams) is "A Servant to Servants," in which the speaker is a lonely and overworked farm wife who talks about her monotonous life to a couple of campers, whose interest in botany has led them to rent tenting ground on her land. It opens with "I didn't make you know how glad I was / To have you come and camp here on our land."

Since a dramatic monologue is a kind of conversation—a one-sided one—conversational diction is called for if the poem is to be believable.

Browning's diction, at least in the poems we have mentioned, does represent the conversation of characters, often of another century, whose philosophic or aesthetic sensibilities have been highly developed. Mr. Sludge is an American; Browning took pains to make him speak in what he took to be American speech of the mid-nineteenth century. Frost, of course, had a more native feel for the speech of his country a half century later.

> Did you ever feel so? I hope you never.
> It's got so I don't even know for sure
> Whether I *am* glad, sorry, or anything.
> There's nothing but a voice-like left inside
> That seems to tell me how I ought to feel,
> And would feel if I wasn't all gone wrong.

Colloquial and substandard as the speech of the farm wife is, the meter is iambic pentameter. So is the meter in the six monologues of Browning we have looked at, though in Browning the speech intonations ride the meter more roughly than they do in Frost. Ever since antiquity it has been suggested that iambic is, as Aristotle said, the "most conversational" of the meters. If any genre particularly demands it, it would seem to be the dramatic monologue. This is the meter that, in pentameter, Williams also uses in his own monologues, although with somewhat more freedom than Frost would allow himself, sometimes dropping syllables, or an entire foot, the meter would like to have, sometimes giving us sequences of freer lines, perhaps out of some emotional urgency or other interest that shakes off the obligations of the meter, as in these lines of the moonshiner:

> When the stuff gets sufficiently hot
> it passes through the aforementioned thumper
> into the aforementioned flake
> whence it drips out a small spigot.

Since Williams shows more freedom in his handling of the traditional meter than Browning or Frost does, it may seem surprising to some that in five of the eight poems we are considering he complicates his metrical structure by adding a structure of rhyme. Browning, who often uses rhyme elsewhere, uses it in only one of the monologues we have referred to, "My Last Duchess," but uses it there in a way that invites us to ignore it, since his run-on couplets glide over it so hurriedly that we are hardly aware of it. This is a device that Williams also uses, so that his rhyme, in most of the poems, is not so conspicuous as to interfere with the conversational rhythms of the sentencing.

In "The Promotion" and "Rituals" he builds a tetradic structure—quatrains, though not printed as quatrains, and frequently run over, as Browning's couplets are. The second and fourth lines of each rhyme. But neither poem closes with a regular quatrain: the first has a rhyming couplet and an unrhymed half line, appropriately expressive; the second closes with a five-line unit rhyming *a x b a b*.

"Missing Persons" is more elaborately structured in consonance instead of in rhyme:

> To judge by what they wore on weekdays,
> he worked in, say, a factory near here;
> she did what sort of thing a woman does
>
> in matching blouse and slacks and flat heels.
> Wait tables, probably, or fix hair.
> They drove a pickup truck with ragged holes
>
> where rust had eaten through, and a fender loose.
> Monday through Friday at seven they rattled west.
> At six they rattled home. In more or less
>
> the time it took him to wash away the grease
> they would come out again. The very worst
> to say about them, across the ragged grass,
>
> is they were beautiful. . . .

The first and third lines of each triplet end with words that have different vowel sounds but keep the same consonant sounds before and after the vowel: *days/does, heels/holds,* and so on. The middle lines of each pair of triplets do the same: *here/hair, west/worst,* and so on. The last unit is a quatrain, its consonance in an *a b b a* pattern.

"*In Extremis* in Hardy, Arkansas" rhymes irregularly but elaborately, in a varying pattern that might recall "Lycidas": now a quatrain, now couplets, now three rhymes perhaps patterned, perhaps not, now rhymes as far as five lines apart. Something similar happens in "The Journalist Buys a Pig Farm," which begins its irregular rhyming when almost halfway through, at the nineteenth of its fifty-one lines. It concludes with two fully rhymed quatrains within its last nine lines.

We have been talking about what might be called the technical specifications of the monologues. Suppose now we look at their substance. Although there are subtle undercurrents and overtones, so that mere plot summaries cannot do justice to the richness of the contents, they can indicate, in oversimplified fashion, the concerns of the poet as shown in the events he chooses to deal with. (1) A businessman, callous if not unscrupulous, tells his dinner guests, a man and wife, how he happened to take over his uncle's company. In passing he gives his comments on such matters as ethics, women, and marriage. (2) To visiting constituents, whom he humors, a senator is frank about the reality of politics, the difficulties of decision making, and, in a changing world that our children will take over, the judgment of history on what we do. (3) Addressing the jury, an attorney admits his client is guilty, but, combining wily choplogic with humanitarian appeals for sympathy, he makes a plea for his acquittal. (4) A waitress talks to a customer about the errors and romantic mischances of her life, which, as it runs downhill, has left her resigned, almost to the point of apathy. But she has known love, if too briefly, and believes that "against appearances / there is love, constancy, and kindness." (5) A person about whom we are told little or nothing gives an officer an account of his neighbors, who lived a mysterious double life of mixed drudgery and glamor that came to an abrupt end with the disappearance of the woman. "But who's to say these facts have any meaning?" (6) A moonshiner, just after the suicide of his brother, a preacher, finds distraction in the realities of his trade, as he describes to a customer the process of making liquor. He concludes by telling his listener how not to get lost as he makes his way home. (7) A ghost appears in a dream to her widowed husband; she describes her insubstantial state as "awareness without form" and wants to assure him, while she still remembers who he is, that things are "alright," that she cared enough to come, and that he should go on with his life. (8) A journalist, disillusioned by the indifference we, and the headlines, exhibit toward the significant ironies of life, and by the relativity of truth, escapes from his profession to a pig farm where he can "read / biographies and listen to old music."

In dramatic monologues, the element of narrative need not be prominent. In those of Williams, as in those of Browning and Frost, the interest lies less in event than in how the speaker feels about event: in the psychological dispositions that brought it about or that were affected by it. Plot receives less attention than character.

Williams's characters are more akin to Frost's farm wife than to the more spectacular figures Browning dramatized. The hardest thing that most of Williams's people have to do is, in the words of the senator, "face the awful fact of the ordinary." Most of them do meet the challenge successfully: they are tough, resourceful, enterprising, or, though disillusioned and down on their luck, they are patient and enduring. "Do what you have to do," the ghost tells her husband; this is the injunction that all of them have the mettle to obey.

In such monologues, the reactions of those spoken to have to be relayed to us by the speaker; all we know about them is what he or she tells us. Some are mere lay figures; they have no character and need none. Browning does report some interaction: Mr. Sludge's antagonist is enraged enough to act; the Bishop's sons seem to stir occasionally and exchange glances; the guards, inclined at first to be rough with Fra Lippo Lippi, relax when he identifies himself as a celebrity and buys them a drink.

In most of the monologues of Miller Williams there is little or no interaction between speaker and listener, though we are free to imagine how the listeners are reacting. Their presence is acknowledged by some of the speakers: the businessman in "The Promotion," for instance, offers to freshen their glasses and calls their attention to a picture—"That's a Magritte that seems to have caught your eye"—just as Browning's Duke points out a piece of statuary:

> Notice Neptune, though,
> Taming a sea-horse, thought a rarety,
> Which Claus of Innsbruck cast in bronze for me!

This is a graceful acknowledgment on Williams's part of his admiration for Browning.

From what we have said already about the protagonists, we know what kind of people they are: how they think and what they think about. What vitalizes their thought is the vigor and raciness with which they express it. They all come from the same world, though from different levels of it; all have the gift of fluency native to a people who have a strong oral tradition.

The earthiness of their speech often has recourse to metaphor. The senator, more literate than most, says,

> You know how the slope of a straight road
> climbing a hill way off ahead of you
> may look like a perpendicular rise.
> You have to get close to see it right.

In this way, he calls attention to the image as a metaphor for seeing better from a distance, and admits there are many other metaphors to say the same thing. The lawyer, speaking of imprisonment as a punishment for the guilty, comes up with an apt analogy from folklore when he recalls the belief that a wound will heal or fester depending on whether the sword that inflicted it is cleansed and sanctified or "buried in corruption." But not only the learned have the gift of vivid imagery; they all have.

Frequently the speakers enrich their language with proverbial folk wisdom: "I knew as much as a dog does about Sunday"; "You can't fall out of a well, so I took chances"; "the kind of girl / that cooks turnips and peas in the same pot." Or, as the moonshiner says when a particularly good batch, even in hard times, calls for a celebration: "A bad year deserves a good day."

Frequently, too, their thoughts are memorable because of the terse and catchy wordplay in which they are formulated: "We measure time by how much time we take"; "He lied not to get, but to get away"; "being scorned and scorning come together / like two ends of a tunnel. Go in at one, / sooner or later you come out at the other"; "Forever is full of now."

The dramatic monologues—though we can see anticipations of them in Williams's earlier work—mark a new stage in his development. What is exciting here is that a poet with nearly three decades of work behind him is finding fresh territories to explore. On the evidence of what he has discovered already, there may well be lavish Golcondas there.

In the First Person
C. D. Wright

There is something uncommonly treelike about certain writers in the South—the way they abide, abide allowing us to prop our backs against the transcripts of their bodies, sparing us all but the weather's worst turns when they are rent themselves. First it is the comely greens and accompanying cools they offer that we appreciate. Eventually we grow to notice the abiding feature of their natures, and it is especially for this we experience lasting gladness.

In the hard-wooded writing of Miller Williams, emphasis is concentrated upon us, our days together, our shared lot. Dominant fears—Madness, Old Age, Death—the poet meets headlong, along with those of lesser clout—loneliness, neglect, forgetfulness. No one is spared, but endurance is built up iamb by iamb. The lives inside the poems mitigate ongoing disappointments by looking at the sunlight as it collects on the bridge, rereading Hardy, remembering the dirty feet of a lover, taking a child's words to heart—inscribing them therein. In other words, the weight of circumstance is lightened by paying attention, by giving a little thanks where a little is due. Always the most elegant case for going on in an imperfect world is an imperfect love.

The instinctual gesture in this writing of love and endurance is to talk matters over, to advise, to hold forth, to inveigh against and exhort. Thus the monologist. And although the monologue does not have the poetic currency it has enjoyed at other points in recent literary history, countless contemporary poets do write an occasional monologue, and a handful of virtuoso practitioners write them in the main. On the side of tradition, Richard Howard and Ai come quickly to mind. On the side of experimentation, Bernadette Mayer and David Antin. Just outside the pale of poetry are the apostrophes of Spaulding Gray and the village recitatives of Garrison Keillor. Though Miller Williams rotates his fields often, the monologue is his staple. Being the son of a preacher, a southerner, and a professor, Williams is by birthright, upbringing, and profession a monologist. Being the son of a preacher, a southerner, a professor, Williams holds his own among the stricter traditionalists, not trafficking in fitful starts on the left side of the margin or arbitrary stops on the right. Evidence the deep-down belief that what one has to say one says within definite limits, that this limitation is as much a matter of propriety as of aesthetics. The line is, else poetry is not. Williams's line stands fast like the break of trees on the slope that keeps the whole area from whirling and washing away.

Furthermore, this traditionalist is writing now at the end of a hysterically technological century, "after the revolution for Jesus," and while he may be determined to retain some of the harder-shelled elements of the tradition, he is swift to offset them with heretical elements. Syntax and punctuation are canonically enforced, while volubility and enjambment allay any apparent rigidity. In place of unyielding banks of anaphora and rhyme, assonantal drifts accumulate. Rhetorical gewgaw is stripped away, and sacred texts are adapted freely. Formal speech is delivered in the form of remarks, albeit final and prepared ones. Therefore, a reckoning is still in order and subjects of sum and substance are there for the reckoning. The upshot is a concinnity of regulation and vernacular, language in check and profusion:

> There are places that even those that live there
> never heard of, places with dictators
> that force democracy on everybody
> and people are poor and dumb and ride donkeys.
> Lord love us all, we don't know what we do.
>
> I needed so much to do something well
> after yesterday and the day before,
> I thanked a woman twice and kissed her hand
> because she said I was a perfect stranger.
> People have loved and left and no one remembers.
>
> The window here could be a clock, Lord love us,
> the way the fields fly by. Sometimes I pray . . .
>
> ("On a Trailways Bus a Man Who Holds His Head
> Strangely Speaks to the Seat Beside Him")

If I ask myself what else becomes of the bardic address in the charge of a secular man before a secular god, I would aver that, however gradually, a newly dreamt, newly clad respect must be reborn. Call it awe. The spirit, be it matter or nonmatter, resists destruction, resists distortion at the hands of abuse, even when magnified by the horrors of history. For the record, if for nothing else, the poet reminds us of our irrelevance among the increments of space, the constellations of time: "Here, unlike forever, it is six o'clock. / The big hand and the little hand, they tell us" ("Rock"). Our frailty: "He prayed but it did not help. It doesn't always" ("Documenting It"). Our fallibility: "Jesus, we're only just got here. / We try to do what's right / but what do we know?" ("Living on the Surface"). Even, alas, our redundancy: "What do we know that matters that Aeschylus did not know?" ("After the Revolution for Jesus a Secular Man Prepares His Final Remarks"). Williams will show these shortages and shortcomings not to discourage us from living out our little lives, which are yet the "inhalations and exhalations of gods," but to charge us to take up the cross of renewal, as it were, under the terms given, to deny nothing and carry on.

Whether Falstaff, Eric-in-the-Evening, the synthesizer through which the mind of Stephen W. Hawking is made manifest and numinous, or Miller Williams waiting for the paper to be delivered, merely musing— nothing craves an audience so totally as a lone person speaking. The audience may hold box seats, be incidentally tuned in, already steeped in the discourse of origins, or just out there. It is a matter of range.

In the monologues of Williams, the voice is unwaveringly direct, the object specific. The speaker's intentions are laid bare. Therefore, the audience is potentially wide though the speaker's cogitations are longhaired. The range of impersonation is broad: "Allende at the End," "Ruby Tells All," "Schumann Adds Trombones to His Second Symphony After Mendelssohn Conducts the First Performance," "In Nashville, Standing in the Wooden Circle Sawed Out from the Old Ryman Stage," "The Picker Has a Vision," "The Ghost of His Wife Comes to Tell Him How It Is," "On a Trailways Bus a Man Who Holds His Head Strangely Speaks to the Seat Beside Him," "The Senator Explains a Vote," and on. It is not ventriloquy that enables Williams to adopt so many personae, for in fact the voice makes minor adjustments, but attentiveness.

With nearly equal frequency the speaker's utterances are Williams's own—man, father, husband, neighbor, citizen, once removed by the fragile mantle of poet, or twice removed by the tentative authority of professor. When related in the past, a welter of related memories usually drives the reader toward a subtle climax: "On my grandfather's farm / there was a river we swam in / there was an old bell to call us back" ("In Your Own Words Without Lying Tell Something of Your Background . . ."). When told in the present the lines all but converge, all but reiterate each other in an effort to illuminate once and forever the speaker's teleological preoccupation. Unsurprisingly these prolonged speeches tend toward a tenebrific density. Here again attentiveness is pressed into service to stay the pain, "When your father dies / take notes / somewhere inside" ("Let Me Tell You"). And, akin to the agitations of Samuel Beckett and William Bronk, the grope toward purpose is unremitting.

Growing up in rural Arkansas, the daughter of a court reporter and a judge, I discovered that my first and most enduring relation to the word has been the law. It is not much of a projection to say that growing up the son of a preacher in rural Arkansas, Miller Williams discovered that his first and most enduring relation to The Word has been The Law. His poems, the monologues especially, reverberate with the perfect attendance record Sundays extracted from his childhood, the Scripture chiseled in his bones. For surely these poems have been summoned out of leather Bibles and board-backed hymnals, out of "the wooden syllables of the South" ("And When in Scenes of Glory"). So in diction, quotations, pulse, and moral deliberation the palimpsest of the homily shows through. It is here that he departs sharply from other monologists more reliant upon dramatic impersonation or narrative. And just possibly it is this rootedness in religion that bestows upon his monologue an abiding treelike nature, up here on the hill in front of Miller Williams's house, where the dozers have left one oak standing, and "Nothing else is vertical on the horizon. / It locks the white sky to the white earth."

 *Tradition and Personal Vision*

Explications of the Poetry

Lewis Turco

One of the most notable features of Miller Williams's style is the tone of the southern preacher, a down-home diction combined with a pulpit rhetoric harnessed to serve an elevated purpose, as in the elegy that is also a prayer, "For Clement Long, Dead," subtitled "lines written in the dark," a poem that the poet unfortunately did not include in *Living on the Surface,* his most recent volume:

> Lord listen, or heaven is undone.
> He will not spell your name or take your hand,
> will hee-haw at the gate with a held breath,
> will run away to the end where death is real.
>
> Lord if you chase him like a wheatfield fire
> till hallelujahs and a choir of angels
> sing him coming and the grand gates open,
> still he will stand against your house
> where no sin ever is and no flesh fails.
>
> If even he has treasures, let the mouse
> discover the grain, take the worm to the tree.
> Give his potential pleasures to the poor,
> or watch him. And watch him well. And watching see
> how he subverts the angels, whispering this:
>
> ninety and nine returned and deserve attending;
> surely the faithful one, the unoffending
> son should have the calf; God, it's a small grace
> to be a counter of coins in the first place.

The images are organic to the poem; although they would be unusual in the mouth of a real preacher, in the lines of Williams they are unobtrusive. The contexts of his poems allow the overtones one associates with the pulpit, but literary associations are not blocked out either, and the poems can be read on two levels—the literal and the allegorical. Williams walks the fine line between rhetoric and symbolism as well as anyone has done during the past quarter century.

If we examine the first poem in *Living on the Surface,* "The Associate Professor Delivers an Exhortation to His Failing Students," we can isolate many of these elements and subsequently follow their development in the body of Williams's work. This piece combines something of the poet's characteristic oratorical quality with what is the major concern of the book, survival. At a glance, the poem appears to be "free verse"—that is, line-phrased prose: each line a phrase or a clause of some kind—but in fact it is a traditionally formal poem in disguise. The typography tells us that the poem is strophic rather than stanzaic; there are twenty-nine irregular sections, some as short as a line in length. Here are the first two strophes—clearly, the professor is a biologist:

> Now when the frogs
> that gave their lives for nothing
> are washed from the brains and pans
> we laid them in
> I leave to you
> who most excusably misunderstand
> the margins of my talks
> which because I am wise
> and am a coward
> were not appended to the syllabus
>
> but I will fail to tell you
> what I tell you
> even before you fail to understand
> so we might in a manner of speaking
> go down together.

An examination of the poem on the sonic level, however, quickly discovers that this is no kind of prose but variable accentual-syllabic prosody. The meter is variable iambics, each line ranging in length from monometer to hexameter:

> Ĭ shoúld ˈ hăve tóld ˈ yoŭ sómeˈthĭng ŏf ˈ ĭmpórtănce
> tŏ give ˈ aͮt leást ˈ ă meáníng
> tŏ thĕ ˈ léttĕr:

> how, after hope, it sometimes happens
> a girl, anonymous as beer,
> telling forgotten things in a cheap bar
>
> how she could have taught here as well as I.
> Better.

The first line of strophe 3 is iambic pentameter verse (see the scansion above), though it has some variations: a promotion of the central unstressed syllable, in a series of three, in the fourth foot and the substitution of an amphibrach in the fifth foot. The next line seems to consist of two iambs and an amphibrach, in that order, and the third line of strophe 3 then looks like two trochees. However, if one were to put lines 2 and 3 together, it would look and scan like this:

> tŏ give ˈ aˇt leást ˈ ă meánˈiňg tŏ̌ ˈ thĕ léttĕr:

In other words, lines 2 and 3 of strophe 3, taken together, are metrically a duplicate of line 1. What we have here, really, is two lines of iambic pentameter verse with falling ends—or, to be descriptively more accurate, iambic hendecasyllabic (eleven-syllable) verse.

Taking a hint from this discovery, we may look back at the beginning of the poem and see that "lines" 1–2 are also equal to one line of iambic pentameter verse, as are "lines" 3–4. The next two combined "lines," however, equal one hexameter, so not everything is going to boil down to pentameter, but it becomes fairly clear that the line-phrasing of the poem is not a strong component of the prosody: rather, it is a disguise of the fact that Williams is writing verse. Perhaps this practice was itself a poetic survival mechanism during "The Great Hiatus" of twenty years and more in American formalist poetry—during the 1960s, 1970s, and early 1980s—when verse-writing was proscribed and only "free verse composition" was allowed.

On the face of things, however, we may say that Williams's prosody in this poem consists of line-phrased, variable, accentual syllabics, and the meter is variable iambics, the range for the lines being from monometer to hexameter. There are great numbers of other sorts of variations in the meters; we can see some of them if we look at strophe 7. Williams substitutes other sorts of verse feet, including anapests,

> The day I talked about thĕ cŏndúcˈtiŏn ŏf cúrˈrĕnts
> Ĭ méant ˈ to say

and an occasional double iamb,

> be care*ful about get*ting hung up in the brain's things

(This line may very well be the thesis of the poem, but more about that a bit later.)

In the beginning of the poem, Williams did not do much with outright rhyme, but there are some line-ending repetitions linking strophes 1 and 2 (*you/you/you* and *misunderstand/understand*); consonances between strophes 2, 3, and 6 (*together/letter/Better*) and within strophe (couplet) 5 (*beer/bar*). True rhyme shows up in strophe 7:

> that send you screaming like madmen through the town
> or make you like the man in front of the Safeway store
> that preaches on Saturday afternoons
> a clown.

This rhyme continues in strophe 8:

> The day I lectured on adrenalin
> I meant to tell you
> as you were coming down
> slowly out of the hills of certainty
> empty your mind of the hopes that held you there.
> Make a catechism of all your fears
>
> and say it over:
>
> this is the most of you . . . who knows . . . the best
> where God was born
> and heaven and confession
> and half of love
>
> From the fear of falling
> and being flushed away
> to the gulp of the suckhole and that rusting gut
> from which no Jonah comes
>
> that there is no Jesus and no hell

This passage is the thesis of the poem stated overtly. The lecturer is delivering a sermon on the subject of religion or the lack thereof in the existential modern world—the associate professor, like Williams, is a biologist and, also like Williams, one of the lapsed and disillusioned faithful. The "failure" here is the failure of both students and teacher, each in the same and different ways. The ideational level of the poem is as important as the sonic.

Returning to a consideration of the latter, we note that from this point in the poem rhyme becomes an important consideration, and it grows as close as couplet rhyme, though more often it is still random (as usual, the emphases are mine):

> that God
> square root of something equal to *all*
> will not feel the imbalance when you *fall*
>
> that rotting you will lie unbelievably *alone*
> to be sucked up by some insignificant oak
> as a child draws milk through straws
> to be his *bone.*
>
> These are the gravity that holds us together
> toward our common *sun*
>
> every hope getting out of hand
> slings us hopelessly outward one by *one*
> till all that kept us common is *undone.*

Rhyme (*sun/one/undone*) links strophes 15 and 16; the latter ends, in fact, in a heroic couplet. As the poem progresses it is pulling together, becoming more and more formal, although Williams has maintained his disguises.

The sensory level of the poem is not complex. The basic tropes are descriptions rather than similes and metaphors. There are more rhetorical tropes than there are images—allusion in particular:

> The day you took the test
> I would have told you this:
> that you had no time to listen for questions
> hunting out the answers in your files
> is surely the kind of irony
> poems are made of
>
> that all the answers at best are less than half
>
> and you would have remembered
> Lazarus
> who hung around with God or the devil for days
> and nobody asked him
>
> anything

The primary schemas are constructional—grammatical parallels mostly—but Williams also avoids punctuation throughout the poem: there are few marks of terminal punctuation, and not many internal ones, either. Williams generally indicates a new sentence or paragraph, as he does in the next strophe, 21, simply with an initial capital letter:

> But if they do
> if one Sunday morning they should ask you
> the only thing that matters after all
> tell them the only thing you know is true
>
> tell them failing is an act of love
> because
> like sin
> it is the commonality within

Now rhyming has progressed to such an extent that the next strophe, number 23, becomes a heroic quatrain consisting of two couplets; Williams says to tell them, that is, the other students,

> how failing together we shall finally pass
> how to pomp and circumstance all of a class
> noble of eye, blind mares between our knees,
> lances ready, we ride to Hercules.

With the puns on "pass" and "class" Williams works his way into the subdued metaphor that has lain dormant throughout the poem till now. This strophe also contains the only overt metaphor of the poem—we are all knights, Don Quixotes de la Mancha, riding out to do battle with Death; we will simultaneously fail and pass on.

Another heroic couplet begins the penultimate strophe 24, which then returns to a semblance of prose:

> The day I said this had I meant to hope
> some impossible punk on a cold slope
> stupidly alone
> would build himself a fire
> to make of me an idiot
>
> and a liar

But the last two lines are now obviously yet another disguised heroic couplet; indeed, if the word *himself* were not present, the last two "strophes" would be another heroic quatrain and might be written out like this:

The day I said this had I meant to hope
some impossible punk on a cold slope
stupidly alone would build . . . a fire
to make of me an idiot and a liar

The poem ends without punctuation, but Williams has asked a question, not made a statement. The mood of the poem is one of disillusion; there is a touch of bitterness in it—gall brought on by a loss of faith—and perhaps of despair staved off at a great cost of will. The viewpoint is dramatic, for, though Williams clearly draws on his own background, he has created a persona who speaks a monologue to an assumed audience of his students. The level of diction is intelligent but not overly intellectual, and the style is mean, not high. If the subject itself is the human intellect, then Williams's thesis is that, though the mind may be an untrustworthy guide through life, intellect is the only guide that mankind has.

The major genre of the poem, then, is dramatics: the specific form is the monologue, though if this were written subjectively it would be a sermon with a strong didactic element. The levels emphasized are the sonic and the ideational, though the typographical is important to Williams's disguise of his prosody, and toward the end of the poem there is heavier emphasis on the sensory. The poem balances the conflict of intellect with mystery extremely well, especially, it seems to me, for an early poem. All, or nearly all, of the elements of Williams's mature style are here, and the poem is a good one for that reason as well as for intrinsic considerations.

"Voice of America," from *The Only World There Is*, finally gives up all technical disguises and announces itself typographically as a verse-mode poem written in quatrain stanzas. Sonically, it is written in normative accentual syllabics—the running foot is iambic and the line length is tetrameter—but as in the earlier poem there are many variations. The rhyme scheme is *a b c b*; thus, the specific form is long measure, from the family of common measure stanzas. It is a cautionary speech in the form of a lyric utilizing the devices we have already noted including repetition and parallelism ("Do not imagine . . . ," begin many stanzas and lines), alliteration, consonance, echo, and assonance.

The sensory level contains, again, primarily descriptions, but there is irony too, and the main image is a simile, "like a bullet hitting a head" the sperm "crashes in" upon the egg to begin the process of reproduction. It appears to be a garish image until, reading closely, we understand that the real comparison is with a rifle bullet entering the head of its victim to finish a life in the same way that life began. The mood of the poem is tense and ominous.

Eventually it will occur to the reader that the subject of the poem is not reproduction but assassination. The schemas Williams uses here are primarily repetitional, the repetitions conjuring up an obsession. The viewpoint is narrative and the syntax is objective—a cautionary tale is being told with illustrations. The level of diction is that of a parent or a teacher (or even a preacher) warning an older child by means of illustrations. The poem, then, is a didactic lyric with a strong narrative element. The levels are in balance—there is even a typographical hiatus in the penultimate line of the eleventh and last stanza to suggest the hole the bullet is making in the head of its victim. This is a poem about the death of John F. Kennedy, or Martin Luther King, or Robert Kennedy . . . or anyone in this world who meets a violent end.

Williams's most ambitious and longest poem, "Notes from the Agent on Earth: How to Be Human," appeared in *Why God Permits Evil*. It seems at first glance to be a verse-mode poem built in both long sections and short—cantos and strophes, with none of the cantos titled. Scansion shows that, indeed, it is verse, normative accentual-syllabic prosody, in fact; the meters are iambic pentameter, but it is not quite blank verse—as in many of his other poems, there is random end-rhyme that at times becomes couplet rhyme, and there are other sorts of sonic devices often taking the place of rhyme, such as consonance and repetition. Williams's jazzy variations haven't changed, either. The general form of the poem is that of the elegy, and the southern preacher inhabits the voice of this poem, as it does in other Williams works, so that at times the poem partakes of the sermon.

There are seven cantos here and, though there are no titles, each of the middle five begins with a parallel: "This is about . . . ." The first canto is an introduction—the scene is Rome, St. Peter's Basilica. The speaker is looking at statuary: Saint Gregory sits on a slab under which "the devil, winged and dog-faced, cat-pawed and crooked / turns in his agony and bares his teeth, / bares his broken claws, turns his nostrils / almost inside out." The last canto is the summation, a coda. It begins, "There is much that matters. What matters most is survival." Williams's lifelong theme is thus stated in so many words. In between the prologue and the epilogue the cantos announce themselves: "This is about Love and how to tell it." "This is about Faith and how to tell it." "This is about the Will to Power, Envy, Covetousness, Ambition."

"This is about Death and how to tell it." "This is also something about Ambition. Also Love. And Faith also. And Death."

Like the earlier poems, on the sensory level "Notes from the Agent on Earth" contains primarily descriptions that sometimes ascend to metaphor, but far outnumbering these are the rhetorical tropes; in particular, Williams here displays a real talent for coining aphorisms:

> Love is Fear and Loneliness fed and sleeping;
> Faith is Fear and Loneliness explained,
> denied and dealt in; Ambition which is envy
> is Fear and Loneliness coming up to get you;
> Death is Fear and Loneliness fading out.

The emotional thrust of the poem is thoughtful tranquillity shot through with neurotic disillusion.

The ideation of the poem revolves around the subject of existence. As we can see, the schemas used are repetitional and constructional, in particular the long parallels of the cantos. The voice here is only partly narrative, for Williams steps out from behind all his masks in this poem to assume the subjective viewpoint and the ego-poetic stance. The syntax follows the form of his thought and only now and again the form of an action. The level of diction is slightly elevated, but the style is mean, not at all florid, though there are some gothic scenes, especially in the prologue. One might be tempted to call the form of the poem georgics, for it is a handbook on how to get through life.

Fusionally, the poem is lyrical and didactic and the levels are balanced, though clearly the ideational is most heavily weighted. For all its preacherly qualities, the poem is most readable, for Williams is ever the musician of language.

In *The Boys on Their Bony Mules* Williams wrote with a greater sense of story. His rhythms and tropes are so well grounded in meter and in the particular that the reader hardly notices the large issue, the thought rising from the poem's base. Williams, despite his scientific background, is one of those poets who were trained, or who trained themselves, in the basics of verse composition and built from that foundation a style of writing and an angle of vision that enabled them to range widely and plunge deeply into the world and the self.

As always in his work, the poems in *Imperfect Love*—formal lyrics and short narratives—consider the human condition in its myriad formations and transformations in such a way as to provide the reader with both insight and delight, as in "A Little Poem":

We say that some are mad. In fact
if we have all the words and we
make madness mean the way they act
then they as all of us can see

are surely mad. And then again
if they have all the words and call
madness something else, well then—
well then, they are not mad at all.

In the same year that saw the publication of *Imperfect Love*, Williams took a role at the forefront of the blossoming neoformalist movement with the publication of his text/anthology, *Patterns of Poetry: An Encyclopedia of Forms*, of which the late John Ciardi said, "Miller Williams has performed a brilliant service in this book. . . . I recommend it to everyone who dares to think he can teach anyone to be a poet." Through this volume's pages the poets of a new generation are beginning again to understand that when a poet writes formally the burden of tradition need not inhibit him in the treatment of the particular subject in hand. This is the true reason that many of the poets of the past two decades have shuddered at the thought of traditional forms: they feel smothered, and indeed they are. But when someone comes along, like Williams, who can understand and release the power of the old constructs in an individual and imaginative manner, the form helps the poet to say the necessary thing.

Miller Williams, then, has done contemporary poetry a singular service in that, during the indulgent decades, he maintained a level of artistry committed both to tradition and to a personal vision. This poetry of balance, of intelligence as well as feeling, will serve as a benchmark to the new generation of poets who are feeling their way back to a sense of writing as literature, not merely self-expression. But his commitment to the craft of poetry takes more forms than just the maintenance of high personal standards. Williams remains the teacher or, if you will, the preacher who exhorts his audience by precept and example. He uses his pulpit to spread the word and the book.

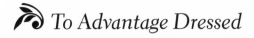 To Advantage Dressed

Miller Williams among the Naked Poets
David Baker

To read the poems of Miller Williams is to brush against the dense, worn, muted fabrics of the world. It is to be asked to fit oneself inside a certain fashion—comfortable, casual, daily—as inside one's favorite work clothes. In fact, if as Alexander Pope asserts in "An Essay on Criticism" it is true that "expression [or style] is the dress of thought," we might find especial value in examining Williams's poetry through its rhetorical methods, its styles, its fashions of expression. In his brilliant *The Motives of Eloquence*, Richard Lanham also engages in this type of project, "to look at words, not through them, to allow ourselves an extraordinary verbal pleasure." He continues:

> So with any detail of dress; it calls attention to, envaluates, an element of structure. It does not try to look natural, look unseen. If it really escaped notice . . . why bother? It wouldn't work. Like a verbal style, it must be seen as such in order to function as an analogue. . . . Thus the whole range of ornament . . . is equally rhetorical, equally deep or equally superficial.

Pope, too, examining the "whole range" of poetic styles, returns to his tropes of ornament and dress to criticize poets he deems unable to portray or re-create simplicity:

> Poets, like painters, thus unskilled to trace
> The naked nature, and the living grace,
> With golds and jewels cover ev'ry part,
> And hide with ornaments their want of art . . .

Likewise, he criticizes those who are unable to control or envalue their abundant, complicated styles:

> Others for language all their care express,
> And value books, as women men, for dress:

Their praise is still—the style is excellent;
The sense, they humbly take upon content.
Words are like leaves, and where they most abound,
Much fruit of sense beneath is rarely found.

Since the publication of his first book of poems, A *Circle of Stone*, in 1964, Miller Williams has worked to develop a distinctive "verbal style" primarily aimed to create an environment of familiarity and acquaintance within the social or public arena. His is a world of surface commotion and texture; his overriding impulse is, persistently, to connect the chaotic, to stitch together the disjointed, to imitate habits of worldly behavior and patterns of public speech. His poetic seems fashioned to allow a rhetoric, a style, whereby he can move easily and comfortably in the world of the human—not to hide nor to transcend nor to boastfully strut, but to facilitate such movement among those he genuinely loves and wonders at: people.

In this regard, Williams's poetic style is quite often diametrically opposed to that of many of his famous contemporaries, poets who have seemed intent on exposing, on defrocking, on stripping away layers of language to reach some primitive, alingual, and either pre- or postconscious truth. I am referring, of course, to the related schools of poets known as the Deep Imagists, the Primitivists, and the Naked poets, that collective group (and its followers) most effectively identified in Stephen Berg and Robert Mezey's anthologies *Naked Poetry* and *The New Naked Poetry*. Especially during the late 1960s and through the 1970s—a period during which Williams published several volumes of his own poetry as well as anthologies, translations, and textbooks—this group attempted to define the limits of simple, stripped-bare style, pushing toward language's very extinction as a way, ironically, to voice social discontent and to mine the self's own antisocial, mystical center. "It is a grammar of departure . . . without any of the comforting associations that had kept the world familiar," as Richard Howard in *Alone with America* says of W. S. Merwin's work. To reject language, to these poets, is to reject society; to extinguish speech with silence is to commune with a ferocious, sublime, unhuman nature. One paradoxical result of such a poetic, of course, is its possible failure *as poetry*—that is, as a kind of language able to be shared—since any transcendental experience may be impossible finally to express in language. Point for point, Williams's project resists the doctrine of the Naked poets as he counters their frequent despair with possibility, their privacy with public connection and concern, and their nakedness with well-fit wisdom. As Pope encourages: "True wit is nature to advantage dressed." Or as Williams states in "Ruby Tells All," to show the natural, hardworking goodness of the speaker as she laments her long-lost daughter:

> She's grown up now and gone though God knows where.
> She ought to write, for I do love her dearly
> who raised her carefully and dressed her well.

"Ruby Tells All" is surely one of Williams's central poems and should serve as an appropriate introduction to some of the signal tendencies of Williams's method. The poem's occasion, its plot, is simple enough. Now in old age, the speaker, Ruby, narrates some of the significant memories of her long life and finds herself wondering about the daughter she bore and raised but who has been gone for years. What Ruby projects into her relationship with her daughter, in fact what she may be worried about in a larger sense than having lost touch with her daughter, is the inevitability of her own death, the growing awareness of her mortality:

> Now, turning through newspapers, I pause
> to see if anyone who passed away
> was younger than I am.

She does not want to leave the world, its people, does not want to lose the thrilling contact—what Whitman calls the "necessary film"—between her body and "those early mornings, waking up . . . the moon full on the fields," when she felt so "important." Ruby is anything but a mystic; she is entirely of this world with its "men who rolled in in Peterbilts," a world where "butterflies turn into caterpillars / and we grow up," and where the possibilities and mysteries of human love are vivifying, rejuvenative:

> There was a man, married and fond of whiskey.
> . . . .
> I would get off work and find him waiting.
> We'd have a drink or two and kiss awhile.
> Then a bird-loud morning late one April
> we woke up naked. We had made a child.

Even nakedness here is a trope to express Ruby's desire to praise her attachment to the world, rather than a means to transcend it. The child, of course, is the daughter for whom Ruby now laments and mourns. What she represents is Ruby's connection to, and her continued and continuing membership in, the world of the human. In addition to the narrative of the poem itself, Williams has charged this poem with other kinds of rhetorical choices that further reinforce Ruby's (and the poet's) connection to the world. He has chosen the method of the dramatic monologue as a vehicle for creating the rich fabric of such a knowing and fond voice as Ruby's, and he has juxtaposed Ruby's rural, uneducated, colloquial diction with the formalizing touch lent by the poem's blank-verse line. In other words, both the voice and the form of the poem—while initially rather contradictory partners—finally serve as effective companions to resist the possibility of Ruby's death. Ruby simply will not be quiet. Nor will the poem, its subject or form, vanish through the kinds of erasures favored by Naked poets such as W. S. Merwin or Robert Bly: "Every morning I forget how it is. . . . I belong to no one," Charles Simic writes. Ruby represents a kind of worldly persistence and presence, a generous faith typical of Williams's poems but quite unusual for Williams's contemporaries. In the poem's final lines, as Ruby catalogs the small and grand gifts of knowledge she would pass on to her daughter, she returns us as well to the controlling trope of my argument:

> What could I tell her now, to bring her close,
> something she doesn't know, if we met somewhere?
> Maybe that I think about her father,
> maybe that my fingers hurt at night,
> maybe that against appearances
> there is love, constancy, and kindness,
> that I have dresses I have never worn.

The figure of clothing here might serve to establish two final aspects of Ruby's strength. She admits that her life has grown abundant and rich, though rich with pains as well as kindnesses; she feels still vibrant enough to want to put on a new dress rather than pass into feebleness or despair or anxiety. Moreover, her return to the metaphor of clothing reaffirms her desire to belong to and in the world of human interaction; her final statement describes her sense of pride, of personal identity, to say nothing of her sexuality and her quiet confidence. She has sent her daughter off well prepared, having "raised her carefully and dressed her well," and she concludes by maintaining her own intent now to send herself back into that world, participatory and wise.

· · · · ·

It should be useful to slow down now and begin to trace more fully the rhetorical strategies of Williams's method that "Ruby Tells All" at least introduces, the strategies of a well-dressed (if rustic) poem, and to contrast these methods with the works of some of the Naked poets. A few lines from W. S. Merwin's "Snowfall" provides an adequate example to begin the comparison:

> Some time in the dark hours
> it seemed I was a spark climbing
> the black road
> with my death helping me up
> a white self helping me up
> like a brother
> growing
> . . . .
> I am beginning
> again
> but a bell rings in some village I do not know
> and cannot hear
> and in the sunlight snow drops from branches
> leaving its name in the air
> and a single footprint
>
> brother

The power of Merwin's best work has always been its sense of mystique, its attempt to negotiate between our failing world and another kind of experience—impersonal, dreamlike, symbolic. He tries to create a mythic, other world perhaps preferable to this one with its Vietnams and Watergates and pollution. Yet, though his work may initially have a social grounding, it generally operates by negation, by removing elements of this world from its canvas. As a result, his poems are often sparsely populated and resound with despair, with a deep longing to transcend and a sense of failure to complete or articulate that transcendence. In *Mythologies of Nothing*, Anthony Libby further defines such a poetic: "It often reflects . . . the medieval *via negativa*; it tends to imagine figural or literal death as the ground of revelation. . . . Often it comes from and leads to nothing." Here in "Snowfall," for instance, we find roads, villages, even brothers; yet these nouns seem to nominate no *recognizable* road, village, or brother. Even the speaker "[does] not know" them. These are instead more like archetypical signs, and our inability to assign specific references to them indicates one aspect of

Merwin's naked style—the impulse to erase references to the literal world and to create in its place an alternative world that often seems populated only by a single speaker and his self-made mythology, a world of types and symbols. "To recur in its purest forms," Merwin has written in a commentary in *Naked Poetry,* "poetry seems to have to keep reverting to its naked condition." The obvious result of a language reverting to its naked condition must surely be silence, the death wish of language. In *The Still Performance,* describing Merwin's longing for such silence, James McCorkle identifies the obvious peril or paradox: "It [silence] is the only thing we cannot accumulate or lose. . . . Silence, however, can only be not-being and the lack of discourse between the self and others."

Miller Williams's poetry, if nothing else, is composed of references to the phenomena and minutiae of this world and to a life lived among a teeming, noisy population. It is the world of people:

> Out of Mobile I saw a 60 Ford
> fingers wrapped like pieces of rope
> around the steering wheel
> foxtail flapping the head of the hood
> of the first thing ever
> he has called his own.
>
> Between two Bardahls
> above the STP
> the flag flies backwards
> Go To Church This Sunday
> Support Your Local Police
> Post 83
> They say the same thing
> They say
> *I am not alone.*

Here, in "Plain," Williams has described a scene in some ways startlingly similar to Merwin's in "Snowfall"—a village with its attendant details and its inhabitants. But the particular differences of those details and inhabitants are equally telling. Williams's speaker travels, not down a *via negativa,* but down a more apparently literal road where people interact. Williams seems fascinated with the names of things specific to this world, and if the Merwin poem presents us with a semiology for his mythic landscape—giving us the signs of the psyche's longing for death and transcendence—then Williams's poem gives us a more literal signification in the images of the bumper and window stickers. They are quite clearly signs of life, signs of work, faith, and *belonging*. They do not accumulate into a mythology, or at least into *only* a mythology; they do not indicate a desire to be transformed or lifted or mortified, to be admitted into the brotherhood of the "white self" or the "snow drop." Yet they do resound with psychic import, albeit an import quite different from Merwin's poem. What they establish is a comfort in the human, a fascination with people, and the significant possibility that art can be made, and comfort found, entirely within the sphere of the this-worldly. Their tacit enemy is silence. Their apparent obligation is to capture or re-create the abundant richness of human and natural phenomena. They include rather than erase: Williams's art is torn from and restitched back into the fabric of the world.

One of Williams's most important poems, "A Poem for Emily," provides us with several more examples of the particulars of the poet's rhetorical methods, and each choice seems again to affirm Williams's resistance of the naked condition and of death itself:

> Small fact and fingers and farthest one from me,
> a hand's width and two generations away,
> in this still present I am fifty-three.
> You are not yet a full day.
>
> When I am sixty-three, when you are ten,
> and you are neither closer nor as far,
> your arms will fill with what you know by then,
> the arithmetic and love we do and are.
>
> When I by blood and luck am eighty-six
> and you are someplace else and thirty-three
> believing in sex and god and politics
> with children who look not at all like me,
>
> sometime I know you will have read them this
> so they will know I love them and say so
> and love their mother. Child, whatever is
> is always or never was. Long ago,
>
> a day I watched awhile beside your bed,
> I wrote this down, a thing that might be kept
> awhile, to tell you what I would have said
> when you were who knows what and I was dead
> which is I stood and loved you while you slept.

Even as he considers the eventuality of his own death, the speaker here is much more intent on praising life, on finding reasons to praise life ("sex and god and politics"); in other words, he resists the elegiac impulse on behalf of the need to establish that "whatever is / is always or never was," to establish the ongoingness of things, as Ruby also articulated her abiding sense of continuity in "Ruby Tells All."

This is not a poem that wants to vanish from the page, that seeks its minimal condition. It suggests itself as a complete artifact rather than a naked archetype. Many of Williams's stylistic choices reiterate this impulse. The rhyme is quirky and memorable, rather like an adult's nursery rhyme; the playfulness of the syntax also serves to make apparent and delightful the rhythmic and alliterative qualities of the language; the five-stress, generally iambic-pentameter lines and the even stanzas establish a formal regularity, a sense of the poem *as poem*— that is, willingly intact within the social traditions of poetry. Williams uses these conventional devices and lends them a rather unconventional voice. Here, as often in his poetry, Williams's speaker finds the language of poetry within the colloquial voice, locates the written within the oral; the lines of the poem are "poetic" lines, and yet the syntax is that of speech. The remarkable sentence that makes up stanzas 3 and 4 is a good example of Williams's marriage of the written and the spoken, the formal and the idiomatic—as the misplaced phrases and entangled zeugmas characteristic of speech wed themselves to the strict lineation. Even this charming and personal voice, I contend, helps to ground the poem's experience in this world, as Williams persists in exploiting the peculiarities of language rather than filtering them out.

Again, a poem by W. S. Merwin will serve as an effective counterpart to Williams's poetic in "A Poem for Emily." The whole text of Merwin's severe, collapsed "Elegy" is as follows:

> Who would I show it to

Where Williams revels in the possibilities of continuity, Merwin laments. His elegy, of course, cannot be an elegy for the death of a person—the way Williams's poem served as celebration of the birth of a granddaughter—for indeed there is no person in the poem. Merwin seems to suggest that the form and/or the impulse of the elegy is itself hopeless or impossible, since the human subject of any elegy will naturally never read that elegy. Rather, Merwin's poem elegizes the elegy, sings a dirge for the possibilities of language itself, turning its failure back on itself.

Merwin's implicit desire to speak to, even to save, the departed must remain unfulfilled since his language cannot be capable of completing the journey to the other world, to death. So it must vanish in its attempt, reverting more and more to the conditions of transparence, of absence, of nakedness.

"Poetry is the wasted breath," Galway Kinnell's note in *Naked Poetry* reads: "The subject of the poem is the thing which dies." Merwin's typical erasure of punctuation, the taut brevity of his utterance, the apparent absenting of personality and contact, the sense that the poem itself is an inadequate translation from another, better condition, all serve to reiterate the poet's desire to transcend experience as the poem vanishes necessarily into silence, into Kinnell's "wasted breath." Conversely, as in "Ruby Tells All," as if to counter the Naked poets' condition of privacy and despair, Miller Williams fills his poems with voices—of aging starlets, associate professors, men on buses, even grandfathers—to find in such populous occasions an encouragement, a means to go on in the world. In the final stanza of another poem, "The Aging Actress Sees Herself a Starlet on the Late Show," the speaker not only seems to answer her own question but also provides a good example of Williams's continued leaps of faith out of despair into connection and persistence:

> How would you like never being able
> to stop moving, always to be somewhere
> walking, crying, kissing, slamming a door?
> You can feel it, millions of images moving;
> no matter how small or disguised, you get tired.
> How would you like never being able
> completely, really, to die? I love that.

To examine more fully the function of imagery in the Naked poets and in Miller Williams demonstrates further the telling differences in their respective poetics and positions. Anthony Libby has rightly identified the "deep image" as one of the most important characteristics of the Naked poets: "The successful deep image strikes with the force of a newly discovered archetype, minor or major, coming from the depths of the poet's subjectivity with a paradoxically universal force, his private revelation made ours." Libby supposes that the poet must "describe his psychic state in images which despite their novelty seem more discovered than made," and may do so by employing "concrete surrealist imagery as the result of 'leaping' from conscious to unconscious mind and back again." Robert Bly's "After Long Busyness" may serve as an adequate example:

> I start out for a walk at last after weeks at the desk.
> Moon gone, plowing underfoot, no stars; not a trace of light!
> Suppose a horse were galloping toward me in this open field?
> Every day I did not spend in solitude was wasted.

Typical of the Naked poets, here Bly recites a list of images that seem elemental, natural, stripped to basics. It is not unimportant that the speaker has been working hard—his writing at the desk, in fact, wants to be seen as parallel to the physical labor of plowing a field— and now has turned to the blank natural world for healing. The wild flight of the horse is his release, his obliteration, and so the totemic images attempt to express his delivery from the tiresome, workaday world into the solitary world where language itself, again, seems inadequate to express "this open field." The images, in fact, suggest a sort of stock formula; they become a set of symbols that leads the speaker from his human self at home, into the dark expanse of nature, and finally, necessarily, into the erasure of "solitude."

Jung must certainly be one of the immediate parents of this poetic. His following passage defines the Naked poets' impulse to discover deep, natural, elemental imagery as a way to locate the absenting spirit or the soul, using the tropes of clothing and bareness to articulate an essentially mystic, transcendental project:

> And if we hide our nakedness . . . by putting on gorgeous robes and trappings . . . we are essentially lying about our own history. It would be far better simply to admit our spiritual poverty. . . . The spirit has come down from its fiery high places . . . but when spirit becomes heavy, it turns to water. . . . Therefore the way of the soul leads to the water, to the dark mirror that lies at the bottom. Whoever has decided to move toward the state of spiritual poverty . . . goes the way of the soul that leads to the water.

Every impulse in Miller Williams's poems resists or contradicts this attitude. If Merwin, Bly, and other Naked poets wish to discover deep images, Miller Williams is thrilled at presenting social images, images raked from the surface of the populous world. It is not inappropriate that he has titled his selected poems *Living on the Surface*. One of his most frequent methods is to assemble disparate images, abundant, even chaotic images, which hardly ever seem to reveal a formula or a means by which to transcend the phenomenal world, "to move toward the state of spiritual poverty," as Jung says above. In other words, his poems are composed of images of the outer world, the tangible, the particular, where inner meaning is relinquished in favor of sheer *being*, where individual identity is not erased but clarified and savored. As if in praise of this very impulse, his "A Toast to Floyd Collins" is a joyous, strange catalog of people, events, and ideas. After toasting the likes of Trotsky and Nicanor Parra, the speaker continues:

> To whoever dies tonight in New Orleans
> To Operator 7 in Kansas City
>
> To the sound of a car crossing a wooden bridge
> To the Unified Field Theory
> To the Key of F
>
> And while I'm at it
> A toast to Jim Beam
> To all the ice cubes thereunto appertaining
> To Jordan knitting
>
> A silver cat asleep in her lap
> And the sun going down
>
> Which is the explanation for everything

This is, it seems to me, a decidedly untranscendental poem, a totally anti-Jungian compilation of images that leads not to the "white spark" of the self but to the social self who loves bodily pleasures such as music, who loves the contact of voices, even the small delights of family, and the making of these things into poetry. He has not stripped away the idiomatic or the impure, as the Naked poets tend to do, but has relished the exotic and the familiar alike, clothing his imagination with the simple material that surrounds him in his daily habitat. Even when those phenomena are not explicable—as, of course, there is in physics no particular formula yet devised for the Unified Field Theory, only the supposition that such a formula may exist—he raises his Jim Beam in praise. The effects here, then, come from the mind's responses to the body's sensations, its delights in the sensory pleasures replete in the world and in the poem. Even the combined images of "Jordan knitting / A silver cat asleep in her lap / And the sun going down" do not, though he says they do, explain anything. The sun's going down cannot be an explanation, only a cause or simply an event. But the speaker knows that; he delights in the irrational, not seeking to transcend a difficult or hard-to-explain existence, happy to feel implicit in the busy, chaotic, surface world.

The impulse of the Naked poets is finally an anti-intellectual one. When Charles Simic states in *The New Naked Poetry* that "poetry is the orphan of silence," he sides with Merwin and Kinnell in his suggestion that poetry is in some essential way a defeated art, that it is unable finally to save itself from obliteration back into silence, or at least that, in trying to resist the merely worldly, poetry must inevitably deny or reject the intellectual processes of the merely human. He continues: "There is a need here, an obsession with purity. . . . In the end, I am always at the beginning. Poverty—an endless condition." The poverty he mentions is surely both Jung's "spiritual poverty" and a poverty of imagination, of language. It is the poverty of mortification that Merwin implies in "Plane," where "my will [is] like a withered body muffled / in qualifications until it has no shape." In this poem Merwin desires "vision of the essential nakedness of the gods" and defines nakedness as "the seamless garment of heaven," again making use of the trope of clothing and nudity to express the issue of humility and selflessness, of the otherworldly.

Williams's poems do not trust the anti-intellectual. He is, more thoroughly, devoted to the thoughtful processes available within the traditions of poetry and of language. His treatment of images should prove his faith in the capacities of the human mind, even the deliberate capacity or decision to resist logic. Where the Naked poets finally distrust the intellectual, choosing instead to obliterate the self and the self's language (language being, of course, an intellectual enterprise), Williams resides entirely in the particular, the individual, and the intellectual—even when he cannot explain a particular phenomenon. Instead of being anti-intellectual, frequently his poems and his schemes of imagery are irrational, finding intellectual delight in their own irrationality. The world is, after all, sufficient for Williams's speakers; they *sense* that it is far larger than they are able to *comprehend*.

In a marvelous example of the world's abundance and a speaker's sense of awe and joy in the irrational, Williams's "Love Poem" is a catalog of apparently unconnected events from around the world and from within the speaker's own neighborhood:

> Six o'clock and
> the sun rises across the river.
> The traffic cop wakes up and
> crawls over his wife.
> The naked professor will sleep another hour.
> The dentist wakes up and reaches for a smoke.

> The doctor reaches for the phone
> and prescribes
> his voice full of rust.
> . . . .
> It is midnight now in Samoa.

As he imagines the unconnected activities of his neighbors, the speaker still creates a connection by the sequences he chooses and by the repetition of words (such as the double "reaches"), the repetition of syntax, and the repetition of events (suggested by the several sleepers as they progressively waken, act, and speak). As the day passes in the poem, the speaker allows his imagination to range into schoolhouses, hospitals, and stores. He follows, or invents, the random activities of his neighbors and juxtaposes these with the passing of time in Berlin, Djakarta, Osaka, and elsewhere, creating a relativist's connection to things. He never wants anything more, never wishes to reject or deny the inexplicable complications and sadnesses of daily human life; instead, as we have seen earlier, he witnesses and names and so ultimately praises. The poem's final lines complete the cycle of the imagined day, returning from their world journey back to the speaker's own home, having traveled but not transcended. The speaker has confronted a chaotic world where "in Mercy Hospital a man is dying" but has as well found a renewed need for love or connection, even if love is irrational, even if life and imagination are limited by time and place:

> Eleven o'clock:
> The children are gone to bed and we are here
> sitting across the room from one another
> accustomed to this house
> that is not ours to keep
> to this world that is not ours
> and to each other.
>
> Sands run through the children in their sleep.

The final possible failure of the deep image is its implication that the phenomena of the world contain a meaning within themselves that is greater than themselves. In writing about James Wright's short-lived but famous phase as a Naked poet, Williams himself identifies the difficulty of such a poetic:

> Leaping . . . requires a symbolic approach to a poem, and so does the deep image, which is simply the sensory end of a leap; both assume that a thing

has an aura of significance beyond its physical fact, or no less important than the fact. . . .
And I suspect that [James Wright] left the leaping alone, on the whole, after *Saint Judas*, because it so easily begins to parody itself.

Williams finds delight and significance in things themselves, in the imaging of things, and seldom strains to invent their psychic or arche-typal meaning. His comment about the availability of the deep image to self-parody is also important, for certainly one of the dangers of the deep image (here interestingly akin to the Puritans' sober and severe *plaine stile*) is the temptation of self-imposed exile, and therefore of narcissism. Recall again Jung's description of the soul, seeking spiritual poverty, as it leans to "the dark mirror" at the bottom of its watery essence. The style of the Naked poets is designed to create simplicity, humility, honesty, sobriety, and probably even to suggest guilt (implied in Jung's "spiritual poverty"). Importantly, this desire to strip away, to unclothe the language, can also turn into a kind of auto-eroticism, a love of the self's ability to appear simple, stripped, nude of contriv-ance, even morally superior. This is precisely the point where the Naked poets finally run into trouble, as Williams predicted above and as Paul Breslin outlines in his article "How to Read the New Contem-porary Poem"—when their plainness becomes a sort of fetish evident in self-plagiarism or unearned drama, when the deep image myth becomes its own subject. This weakness is certainly to be found in recent work by some of the poets I have used here to represent the Naked poets. Since the mid–1970s their work has too often turned into a kind of rhetorical narcissism, as if they have fallen in love with their own naked, mortified selves. The unfortunate result is that their per-sonal agonies and transformations ring untrue and do not, as Libby says they must, turn their "private revelation[s]" into ours.

Williams seems to identify explicitly the danger of transcendence, the failure of the private revelation to connect, in "One Day a Woman":

> One day a woman picking peaches in Georgia
> lost her hold on the earth and began to rise.
> She grabbed limbs but leaves stripped off in her hands.
> Some children saw her before she disappeared
> into the white cloud, her limbs thrashing.
> The children were disbelieved. The disappearance
> was filed away with those of other women
> who fell into bad hands and were soon forgotten.
> Six months later a half-naked man in Kansas

working on the roof of the Methodist Church
was seen by half a dozen well-known
and highly respected citizens to move
directly upward, his tarbrush waving,
until he shrank away to a point and vanished.
Nobody who knew about the first event
knew of the second, so no connection was made.
The tarbrush fell to earth somewhere in Missouri
unnoticed among a herd of Guernsey cows.

While I do not want to go so far as to claim that Williams wrote this poem *about* the Naked poets, still the details of the poem certainly give us plenty of invitation to read it as such. The woman's disappearing in a "white cloud" while working in her perhaps Edenic garden, the "half-naked man" who moved "directly upward" while tarring his church with a brush (like an artist's tool), the absurdity of the pious, pure situations, all point to Williams's tacit attitudes toward art-as-transcendence. Such privacy fails to become valid as a possibility for art, since "no connection was made." Over and over, Williams's poems desire connection over transcendence, delight over despair, the pleasures of verbal texture and formal fabric over nakedness and simplicity.

• • • • •

The conflict described here, between the style of Miller Williams and that of the Naked poets, is not new to the contemporary realm. Nor is it limited among the contemporary scene to these poets only— for certainly we could usefully see the works of Howard Nemerov or Richard Wilbur as sympathetic to Williams's aesthetic, and many of the works of Peter Everwine or James Dickey (a southerner, like Williams, but worlds apart from Williams's poetic) as essentially transcendental in the manner of Merwin, Bly, or Kinnell. Still, it might be useful in conclusion to outline some of the traditions within which Williams's worldly vision operates, as well as those that foreground the Naked poets' impulses.

The conflict, as I see it, is most probably the conflict between Philip Rahv's "palefaces and redskins." Or, to avoid Rahv's unfortunate racism, it is the conflict in America between Eliot and Robinson, or earlier between Emerson and Twain, even between Edwards and Franklin. It is probably traceable to the very deep, essential tension between Platonic and Aristotelian inclinations—that is, to the most basic rift in Western thought.

To the Puritan in Edwards, the transcendentalist in Emerson, and the modernist-turned-mystic in Eliot, the function of language is ultimately otherworldly, Romantic, Platonic. Its impulse is to resist and deny or despise the public, to develop the private and the self-reliant, in order to allow the individual a means to transport himself away from this world. Its components include a transparent or naked language, high seriousness or morality, associative leaping, and objects loaded with spiritual, symbolic significance. This literary philosophy, like most religions, is markedly sublime, and as Thomas Weiskel observes in his *The Romantic Sublime,* "the essential claim of the sublime is that man can, in feeling and in speech, transcend the human." Harold Bloom identifies, in his *Ruin the Sacred Truths,* two of the greatest difficulties in such an aesthetic:

> Transcendence of the human in speech, particularly in the utterance within a tradition of utterance that is poetry, necessarily relies upon the trope of hyperbole, an over-throwing ... that is closer to simplification through intensity than it is to exaggeration. Transcendence of the human in feeling is a universal experience (or illusion) and itself transcends most modes of utterance.

We have identified the dangers of "naked" simplification in Merwin's work and have also explored the paradox that a transcendental experience itself transcends our capability to express it. Nakedness is simply not enough, as Richard Lanham complains: "Naked into the world [we] came, *but not without resource.*"

In the other camp, to the Deist in Franklin, the social humorist in Twain, and the formal realist in Robinson, the function of language is this-worldly, and thereby classical, Aristotelian. Its impulse is to participate in the public discourse, to revel in and learn from the things of this world, to admit the irrational and the particular, even the peculiar, and to remain at last "well-dressed" in the public's presence by making use of ornament and the personalizing intricacies of style. It will not erase but employ and relish the peculiarities of human experience and behavior. Again, Lanham defends this aesthetic with clarity and precision: "Ornament, in a way then, seems more honest than plainness. It does not affect a naturalness in the nature of things unattainable. . . . The way to naturalness lies through artifice, not around it." The corollary ingredients of this aesthetic and style may include colloquial and idiomatic language, humor, practical or worldly knowledge, images that resist merely symbolic significance, experience that resists the otherworldly or the merely private, and the willing inheritance of traditional formal and/or narrative structure. This literary philosophy is decidedly untranscendental; and it is Williams's home.

As if directly to confront the temptation to vanish into a Naked poet's typical landscape, Williams's poem "Waiting for the Paper to Be Delivered" gives us a final, ample example of this poet's vision and faith:

> Late January.
> Snow is on everything.
> No matter how far I listen there is only silence.
>
> Two yellow machines have worked for a week
> cutting away the hill in front of the house
> I have come to live in for the rest of my life.
>
> On the highest part of the hill
> one oak is standing.
>
> Nothing else is vertical on the horizon.
> It locks the white sky to the white earth.

Though he hears only silence, he is, importantly, waiting for the news of the world to be delivered. The silence of line 3 is immediately subsumed by the human commotion implicit in the second stanza. Time and again, Williams resists Merwin's erasure, his "white self." We find here instead remarkable assurance in the one oak standing "on the highest part of the hill." Though he says the oak "locks the white sky to the white earth," it must also surely be true that—like a pencil propping open a window, or like the poet's own desire—the oak also keeps the two clearly apart. It keeps the speaker safe to live in his house "for the rest of [his] life." Like a good winter coat, buttoned and well fit, this poem takes its speaker out into the spare landscape and lets him come back, alive.

III

A POEM FOR EMILY

Small fact and fingers and farthest one from me,
a hand's width and two generations away,
in this still present I am fifty-three.
You are not yet a full day.

When I am sixty-three and you are ten,
and you have known me ~~~~
~~~~
~~~~
~~~~arithmetic~~~~

When I by luck and blood am eighty-six
and you are some place else and thirty-three
believing in sex and god and politics
with children who look not at all like me,

some time I know you will have read them this
so they will know I love them and say so
and love their mother. Child, whatever is,
is always or never was. Long ago,

a day I watched a while beside your bed,
I wrote this down, a thing that might be kept
a while, to tell you what I would have said
when you were who knows what and I was dead
which is I stood and loved you while you slept.

 *Miller Williams, Translator*

It has been over fifteen years now, but I can remember the January evening vividly. A dozen or so of us gathered in Miller Williams's living room in Fayetteville for the initial meeting of a course that was being offered for the first time, a workshop in literary translation. The setting itself was familiar; since coming to the University of Arkansas in 1970, Miller had regularly met the poetry workshop in his home—on the one hand a concession to the bad back that must have made three hours in a classroom chair an ordeal for him and, on the other, an indication of his sincere desire to make his students comfortable in what, for those who had never quite gotten used to having their poetic effusions picked apart by their peers, was never a particularly relaxing situation. The three or four students there who had taken Miller's poetry work-shops were familiar with both his hospitality and his methods. True, we were all on a first-name basis and could smoke and drink and discuss freely, but it went without saying that some proprieties would be observed. Voices were rarely raised, and one could expect to be heard out without interruption. Miller usually had the last word, as was fitting, and in the low, somewhat hesitant voice that is his trademark he would offer final judgments on the poems that were not often contested. Though we usually chafed at his criticisms, in retrospect they seem to have been mild and tempered with more courtesy than either we or the poems deserved. He was open to a wide range of poetic strategies from the traditional to the experimental, and he exercised solid common sense in his readings. He brought, in the best sense of an often misused word, a *disinterested* quality to bear on the workshop drafts, the eye and ear of a skilled editor who could spot weaknesses that kept a poem from fulfilling its potential.

That night, however, there was a general air of uncertainty in the room. The course was new, one that was perhaps unique in American academia. We wondered how we would proceed in a class in which the material under discussion would conceivably span centuries, several genres, and different languages. Those of us who had come into the class from the creative writing program immediately felt at a disadvantage, with our undergraduate work in Spanish or German largely forgotten and our crash courses in Ph.D. French making us barely capable of getting through a page of *Candide* without at least one howler. Here were graduate students from the modern languages curriculum and a couple of native speakers of foreign languages whose English was often more correct than ours. Like the apocryphal *turistas* who ordered *te frito* in restaurants and tried to exchange their *dolores* for the native currency, we knew that one is never so open to outright ridicule as when he misuses a language not his own. I recall that later, when a student translated a phrase from one of Baudelaire's prose poems as "your elastic and unwieldy hair," Miller gently suggested that *yielding* and *heavy* might be more appropriate modifiers. On the other hand, the foreign language students must have felt similar apprehension at what they were about to embark on; skilled as they may have been with literal translations of textbook examples, many of them had never attempted an original poem or story before.

Miller Williams was, and remains, a skillful organizer. He quickly outlined procedures that would get us through the course with a minimum of confusion. In offering a translation to the workshop, each member would provide a copy of the original, a "trot" or literal translation (either his own or from another source like a bilingual text), and his own version. Miller had anticipated that our linguistic abilities would be unequal, and he quickly made it clear that the finished translation, arrived at by whatever means we had at our disposal, would be the main focus of our discussion. The language experts in the class could debate the finer points of meaning, and the creative writers could likewise discuss the translations' merits as texts in their own right. These were the sorts of accommodations, we were shortly to learn, that were necessary in the treacherous no-man's-land of literary translation. Copies of several versions of Dante (Longfellow's, Binyon's, Sayers's, and Ciardi's) were passed around, and we discussed some of the obvious problems in translating poetry. A dogged literalism had advantages for the scholar, but it could hardly be said to yield an English version that "carried across" (the literal sense of the word *translated*) the effect of the original as a native reader would experience it. At the other extreme, we discussed the pitfalls of playing too freely with the original text. Lowell's *Imitations* was still newsworthy and controversial, and the secondhand influence of Spanish surrealism could be seen in a number of recent books and in poems from the poetry workshop. It was implicit from his remarks that Miller had little patience with the then-current vogue of translating poems that were rhymed and metrical in the original into the free-verse paraphrases that were widely applauded as adequate versions. *Compromise* was the term that surfaced most commonly and without apology. Some sense of the original's formal qualities had to be brought over without doing undue damage to its literal sense. In many ways, Ciardi's version of Dante, with its relaxed measures and reduced rhymes, became the paradigm of a work in which, to use Richard Wilbur's phrase, the translator places himself "in the service of" the poem. These same balanced standards have, I think, served Miller well in his own translations.

It may come as a surprise to some to learn that Miller Williams has no academic credentials as a linguist. As a young man, he was tutored in Latin by his father, a Methodist minister, but his undergraduate and graduate work was in the sciences and he began his academic career as an instructor of biology. It was probably the influence of John Ciardi, who was instrumental in assisting Miller's early career as a poet and who remained a lifelong friend and advisor, and that of John Nims, the poet and translator whom Miller first met at Bread Loaf in 1962, that turned him toward literary translation. As Miller has remarked on numerous occasions, "It was Ciardi who first showed me that a translation could have a life of its own as a literary work." An Amy Lowell Traveling Fellowship allowed him to live in Chile in 1963 and 1964, and it was there that he became enough at home in Spanish to translate the work of a number of Chilean poets and playwrights and then to teach, as a Fulbright lecturer, in Mexico City in 1970. The Prix de Rome, awarded in 1976, brought him a year's residence at the American Academy in Rome, where he quickly learned both standard Italian and the Romanesco dialect. Further travels, often undertaken as a government lecturer, have familiarized him with French and German as well. Miller is quick to point out that his classrooms, more often than not, have been the cafés, bodegas, and coffee shops of the countries where he has resided. These intimate contacts with the *spoken* language have served him well with the two poets he has chosen to translate most extensively, Nicanor Parra and Giuseppe Belli.

During his year's residency in Chile, Miller met many of the poets and playwrights of roughly his own age whose work he would later collect and, in most cases, translate in *Chile: An Anthology of New*

Writing, but it was his friendship with Nicanor Parra that would prove most fruitful and lead to the publication of two collections that have made Parra one of the best known of all South American poets among American readers. Born in 1914, Parra stands almost exactly halfway between the generation of Pablo Neruda (b. 1904), Chile's dominant Modernist poet, and that of Miller himself. In 1960 Parra had published *Discursos,* jointly written with his mentor Neruda, which looked both backward in its discussions of the elder poet's influence and forward in hinting at directions that younger poets might take. Parra's own "antipoetry," which had begun to appear in print in the late 1930s, remained controversial and decidedly avant-garde. Its flat, understated idiom and surrealistic dislocations had led at least one critic to state, "It's too dirty to be immoral. A garbage can is not immoral, no matter how you turn it." Miller himself, fresh from the controversies swirling in American poetry in the early 1960s, made an apt comparison: "The Beats belonged to our time, and they had in their own language a precedent; still [they] were met with calumny. Parra is establishing his own precedent. He calls it antipoetry. It has shaken the rigid structure of poetic theory and challenged old critical concepts with such force that virtually every writer and literary scholar in Latin America is ready to attack or defend it." The analogy with the Beats is well taken; the only earlier translations of Parra's work were a small selection published by Lawrence Ferlinghetti's City Lights Books in 1960. In bringing Parra's work to a wider American readership, Miller was anticipating the influence of South American writers on the work of such diverse North American poets as W. S. Merwin, Mark Strand, Robert Bly, and James Wright.

But I suspect that, more than anything, it was Parra's personality and background that established such close bonds between himself and his young American translator. Like Miller, Parra was trained as a scientist, eventually becoming professor of theoretical physics at the Instituto Pedagogico of the University of Chile in Santiago. Having studied in the United States at Brown University, he was bilingual and cosmopolitan and, as we students observed during his visit to the University of Arkansas, a man of eminent sociability and personal grace. One can hear, in the direct conversational idiom of Miller's early poetry, similarities between his own concerns and Parra's that must have made them naturally *simpático.* Parra's pride in the careers of his sister Violeta and his nephew Angel as folk musicians parallels Miller's own fascination with this subject and his long-standing support of his daughter Lucinda's musical career. While Miller was preparing the manuscript of *Poems and Antipoems* in Baton Rouge, Parra served briefly as a visiting professor at Louisiana State University—a closeness, both personal and professional, that led to the successful publication of both the first book and the subsequent *Emergency Poems* by New Directions, a publisher whose influence, on younger poets in particular, has been immense.

Commenting on the work of another American translator, Richard Wilbur, in an essay published in the *Sewanee Review* in 1984, I began with some general observations:

> Translating poetry is a task of such supreme difficulty that one wonders why poets continue to attempt it. Not only must the poet relinquish his own identity while serving a term of apprenticeship to the mind and will of another; he must also satisfy readers who are more critical in their readings of translations than they are in dealing with original poems. One critic chastises the translator for his lack of fidelity to the exact letter of the original text; another deems his formal reconstructions flawed; while yet another complains that the translator does everything but reproduce the *voice* of the original poet. Not only must a translator walk the tightrope of meaning while simultaneously juggling meter and rhyme, but he is expected to provide vocal impressions as well. Good poetic translation must make the best of a bad compromise between languages in the same way that treaties between nations must weigh the numerous variables that separate one culture from another. The poet who translates well is truly a diplomat who allows one unacknowledged legislator to communicate with his peers around the globe.

In a recent book, *The Art of Translating Poetry,* Burton Raffel distinguishes four main types of poetic translation: (1) *formal,* a literal reading aimed more at scholars than at general readers; (2) *interpretive,* aimed at a general audience that reads for literary reasons; (3) *expansive,* aimed at readers "who usually prefer to read something, anything, new rather than anything old"; and (4) *imitative,* aimed at an audience that wants the work of the translator rather than the work of the original poet. Miller's translations of Parra, it seems to me, combine elements of the first three of these; in insisting on bilingual texts in all of his translations, Miller allows the linguist to compare the exactness of the version with the original, and he has managed to produce translations of Parra that should please both those who are reading the poems as translations and those who want to read poems that are good in their own right. In all of his translated work, he has resisted the temptations of loose imitation; he would shudder at the thought of violating both letter and spirit of original texts in the way, say, that Robert Lowell did. A translation by Miller Williams is just that, a *translation*, not an excuse for pilfering the word hoard of another poet.

On a superficial level, Parra presents relatively few impediments to one who would render him in English. For the most part his poems are in open forms, and his idiom is simple and unadorned. His syntax is straightforward, and whatever ambiguities arise in his poems stem from their overall meanings rather than from obscurity in language. This surface lucidity, what we may term a poetic version of the architectural International Style, is classical, almost Doric, in its unadorned facade. As Miller notes in his introduction to Parra, "As much as anyone writing, and far more than most, Parra is a poet of surfaces. Because poetry, an attack on the senses, is a game of surfaces, that being all the senses know about. And Parra knows, anyway, that even metaphysically the surface of things is the proper concern of poetry, because the masks and dyes and ways of walking tell more of the heart than we can find out with a flashlight in its darkest corners." This transparency of surface effects, in many cases, presents the translator with few apparent difficulties, as parallel passages from Parra's "Sueños" and Miller's version, "Dreams," illustrate:

> Sueño con una mesa y una silla
> Sueño que me doy vuelta en automovil
> Sueño que estoy filmando una pelicula
> Sueño con una bomba de bencina

> I dream of a table and a chair
> I dream I go for a spin in a car
> I dream I'm filming a movie
> I dream of a gas station

One notes that the lines of Miller's version are syllabically shorter than those of Parra's, a concession to the monosyllabic nature of the English spoken vocabulary; certainly nothing could be gained by replacing *automovil* with its English cognate. But even a single example like this illustrates the range of options the translator has at his disposal, our language possessing more alternatives to saying a given phrase than almost any other. Thus, Parra's phrase "filmando una pelicula," rendered here as "filming a movie," appears as "shooting this picture" in a translation of Parra's "Pido que se levante la sesion" ("I Move the Meeting Be Adjourned") by Allen Ginsberg, one of the other translators whose work appears in *Poems and Antipoems*. The only dif-

ference in Parra's two uses of the phrase arises from his use of the
indefinite article *una* in the first and the definite *la* in the second.
Ginsberg's choice of carrying over cognates leads to an English version
of "No veo para que / continuamos filmando la pelicula:" that sounds
stilted: "I see no reason / To continue shooting this picture!" These are
small matters, to be sure, but one wonders about such choices as "continue" where "keep" would do, "this" for Parra's "the," and the substitution of an exclamation mark for the original colon. These represent licenses, however minuscule, that Miller rarely takes with Parra's
lines. If, on occasion, the syntactical differences between Spanish and
English force the translator into clear compromises, Miller's judgments seem like wise ones. This brief example from "Nieve" should
suffice:

> Empieza
> a
>   caer
>   otro
>   poco
>   de
>   nieve

A literal rendering, "Begins to fall another bit of snow," sounds false to
the English ear. And what is one to do with the subtle *visual* dimension
of Parra's poem, which approaches some of the "concrete" effects of
E. E. Cummings? Miller's version, with its natural syntax and revised
spacing of the two shortest English words, provides a close equivalent
which, incidentally, is a perfectly scannable line of iambic pentameter:

> A
>   little
>   snow
>   is
>   starting
>   to
>   fall
>   again

If, in saying that Parra's poetry presents the translator with "few apparent difficulties," I give the impression that he is easy to translate, I
should here add that the *unapparent* difficulties of poetic translation
are, in most cases, what escape the eye and ear of the mediocre translator. Reading over Miller's translations of Parra for the umpteenth

time in twenty years, I still fail to discover any cases where his instincts are not proved correct. When he departs from the letter of the original, it is usually for the reader's benefit. Here is one more example, from Parra's "La doncella y la muerte" ("Death and the Maiden"):

> La doncella rolliza
> Toma una flor que hay en un florero
> Y se la arroja a boca de jarro.

The maiden is flirting with Death, who throughout the poem does nothing in response until, in the last line, "he takes her." This short passage presents a number of difficulties. Literally, it is almost untranslatable: "The plump maiden takes a flower that is in the flowerpot and hurls it at him to the mouth of a jar." The problem lies in the secondary meaning of *arrojar* ("to shed blood") and in the idiom *a boca de jarro*, which implies "point blank" or "wide open" with a suggestion, in some contexts, of suddenness and lack of forethought. Here is a prime example of something that Miller has stressed in his translations and teaching repeatedly, that is, that we cannot *read* in English what was *written* in another language. The translator must of necessity decide what the poet *would have said* if English had been his primary tongue. Miller's translation is a model of economy that nevertheless carries across the ironic tone of this absurdist allegory:

> The maiden is round of body
> And suddenly in cold blood
> Throws a flower at him.

In this one hears the underlying seriousness that plays through centuries of poems on the carpe diem theme. In its own way, it is as elegant and as chilling as Marvell's "The grave's a fine and private place, / But none, I think, do there embrace."

I hope to have illustrated a paradox that confronts the translator of Parra. The precise, clear surfaces of Parra's poetry at first glance seem to invite translation. The translator does not have to replicate meter and rhyme, and he is faced with few examples of verbal ambiguity. However, Miller has noted that these beguiling features can soon turn to the translator's disadvantage: "One quickly learns," he has said, "that the translator of, say, Neruda can immerse himself in that poet's lyricism. To his dismay, Parra's bare, unadorned language literally leaves him no place to hide." In other words, the simpler the surfaces of the poems, the less leeway the translator has in transposing them to what Wilbur calls "equivalent effects in the key of English." Indeed, any foreign poet posits a new set of variables for his would-be translator, and Giuseppe Belli, whose sonnets Miller began to translate during his year in Rome, presented entirely different challenges.

No one can accuse Miller Williams of standing still as a poet. His first books were largely in open forms. In the second half of his career, the beginning of which is marked roughly by the publication of the selected poems in *Halfway from Hoxie,* he has experimented boldly with the forms and meters of the tradition, a direction that led to the publication of his dictionary of poetic forms, *Patterns of Poetry.* In attempting to translate Belli, he faced immense difficulties, three of which seem to me most prominent. First, Belli wrote in Romanesco, the dialect of Trastevere. In addition to learning standard Italian, Miller as well had to become at ease in this "people's language," which has common ancestry with Italian but is not, properly speaking, a dialect of it. Second, Belli's poems are written in that most demanding of poetic forms, the so-called Petrarchan sonnet with its *a b b a a b b a* octave. English poets since Wyatt and Surrey have noted that English, with its relative paucity of rhymes, is no match for the inflected Romance languages here. Third, and perhaps most important, Belli, who lived from 1791 to 1863, which is to say roughly contemporaneously with the second generation of English Romantics, has a unique voice for which there is no analogy in the English tradition. He is satirical, coarse, and often obscene, and no English poet, not even Byron, would have dared express the scandalous opinions on government, the Church, and human nature that fill his poems. Additionally, he has not been widely translated into English; a few fugitive pieces by Eleanor Clark, in her *Rome and a Villa,* and other versions by Harold Norse and Anthony Burgess represent only a few of the roughly two thousand sonnets that Belli wrote. In many ways his poetry represents a great unknown quantity for the translator.

Belli merits three sentences in the *Encyclopedia Britannica.* Though the Roman people have long recognized him as "their" poet and indeed erected a statue to him in gratitude, his reputation, even among his admirers, has always been as a "low" poet, fit for tavern recitation but hardly appropriate for serious study. His anticlerical stance outdistances even Rabelais's and would probably still shock the pious reader. His life is filled with personal contradictions, not the least being his longtime service as an official Vatican censor and his remarkable turn from liberalism to arch conservatism following the upheavals of 1848.

Finally, this most indefatigable of sonneteers ordered—in vain—that his poems be destroyed after his death; they did not appear until the 1880s, when Luigi Morandi's six-volume edition was published.

As Miller makes clear in his translator's note, several compromises had to be made at the outset, the most prominent being "the free use of slant rhyme to represent the true rhyme of the original" and "the use of separate rhyme-sets for the octave," *a b a b c d c d* instead of the original's *a b b a a b b a*. "There was never a thought," he goes on to say, "of abandoning rhyme ... partly because I like the way a sonnet's external pattern confirms its internal logic, [and] partly because I think a sonnet without rhyme has about as much appeal to sense and the senses as a bird without feathers." Instead of Belli's strict hendecasyllabics, the Italian equivalent of our pentameter, Miller substitutes a five-stress accentual line. Concerning an appropriate idiom for the dialect, the rule of common sense applies: "If we are to come to [the sonnets] as the people of Trastevere did, then we have to hear them as they did, in the plain language of their own conversation. The simple fact is that, to those who live in Trastevere, the language spoken in Trastevere is the way people talk."

These compromises proved to be wise ones. There is just enough of the form left to make the satire sharp:

> We were molded out of garbage and turds,
> you know we were, before we made our entry
> into this world. All those other words,
> decorum and merit, they're something for the gentry.

The relaxation of the meter allows a voice to emerge that speaks in idiomatic English:

> Look at my grandmother's beauty: a foot of skin
> hangs around her neck. It's full of lumps,
> like raisin pie; it shakes like leaves. That hole
> she calls a mouth can nibble a few crumbs.

All this is accomplished, if I can rightly judge by comparing Miller's versions with those of other translators, with minimal sacrifice of the literal sense of Belli's lines. Belli is a realist, often brutally so. His imagery, when he is not rewriting the Bible, sounds surprisingly modern; in "Kitchen Stuff" the speaker buys "a copper coffee pot, a set of weights, / a three-legged stool, a bellows, a pasta table" from a widow at a flea market. "This was all stuff her husband had. / He was a palace cook;

one of the princes / left the kitchen to him when he died." In "A Bad Moment" the horror of a father and son at finding a dead girl "close to where the whorehouse throws its trash" is still remembered by the son years later: "I go out on picnics and sit there / and never hear what anybody says." On Belli's mean planet there is little room for the kind of idealism we usually identify with the Romantic period: "Look at kittens, my friend. We always keep / the prettiest ones to raise. And the ugly runts? / The ugly runts end up in the garbage heap." It should come as no surprise that, according to Miller's introduction, Gogol and Joyce were among Belli's admirers.

Belli is at his best, and Miller is likewise, when satirizing biblical subjects. Reading these translations, I cannot help being reminded of the mordant humor of Miller's "Why God Permits Evil." Even Paradise is tainted: "Then Adam came and made himself the boss, / with an executioner's axe and a blunderbuss." The Earthly Paradise, compared with the Roman streets of Belli's day, must have seemed remote indeed. All Belli can manage is a sour understatement in his summary of life in *la bella Roma:* "The living, all said and done, the good and the bad, / just by being alive, if nothing else, / are doing somewhat better than the dead." Discovering Belli in these translations causes one to redefine any previous concept of the poetry of the period. It is small wonder that Richard Wilbur singled out *Sonnets of Giuseppe Belli* as one of 1981's most remarkable poetic events.

I know neither Italian nor Romanesco, so it would be pointless to provide one of Belli's originals here (besides, they are readily available in Miller's collection). But it is instructive to look at what happens in the process of turning literal trot into poetic translation. Here is the first draft of "Abraham's Sacrifice, II":

> After having a little breakfast
> all four left at daybreak,
> and walked, praying all the time,
> for forty miles more than a hundred.
>
> "We've arrived: this is it," said the big old man.
> "Strap on the bundle, dear son";
> then turning to the houseboy, he said:
> "Wait here with the donkey."
>
> While Isaac climbed, he was saying, "Papa,
> tell me, where's the victim?"
> And he answered: "A little further ahead."

> But when they finally got to the top,
> Abraham screamed at his son: "Isaac, you
> get your face to the ground. The victim is you."

This may be accurate enough, but it does not rise above bare paraphrase. Yet many contemporary translators might have been content with this first draft, feeling that to impose rhyme and meter on the prose sense of the poem would be to violate it. Miller's skill here is apparent when we look at his final draft. The changes he makes are actually small, and what he eventually achieves adds the closure that can come only through retaining elements of the sonnet form:

> They had a little breakfast, and then all four
> started walking at daybreak. All of them prayed
> every step of the way, and they went for more
> than a hundred miles when the old man stopped and said:

> "We've got to where we're going. This is the place.
> Strap on the wood, son." And then he turned
> to the servant boy: "I want you and the ass
> to wait here till the sacrifice is burned."

> Halfway up the mountain, Isaac said:
> "My father, where's the victim for the Lord?"
> His father answered: "A little further ahead."

> But when the climb was over and those two
> were standing alone at the top, Abraham roared:
> "Your face on the ground, son; the victim is you."

Since the publication of *Sonnets of Giuseppe Belli,* Miller has continued to translate and, despite his other obligations as a poet and as director of the University of Arkansas Press, to direct the translation workshop occasionally. To return to my opening recollections, I might remark that, among many other measures of his skills as a translator and as a teacher, the course in literary translation is now permanently established at the University as the cornerstone of its M.F.A. in Translation degree program, the only one of its kind in the United States. Among those who have taken the course and gone on to translate poetry, I might single out John DuVal, whose *Cuckolds, Clerics, and Countrymen* is a classic version of medieval French fabliaux, and Sandra Reyes, first winner of the American Literary Translators Association's prestigious Richard Wilbur Prize. Perhaps only those who themselves translate poetry can fully appreciate Miller Williams's accomplishments in this field, but I suspect that thousands of readers will remain indebted to him for his efforts. His translation of Parra's "Jovenes" provides an appropriate coda to these remarks:

YOUNG POETS

Write as you will
In whatever style you like
Too much blood has run under the bridge
To go on believing
That only one road is right.

In poetry everything is permitted.

With only this condition, of course:
You have to improve on the blank page.

 *Of Devils and Saviors*

Gabrielle Burton

Bread Loaf, 1972. Maybe because it was a strange, spooky place, an isolated mountaintop filled with moody, desperate, volatile writers (it was after all the only writers' conference whose application had a space for your psychiatrist's number), or maybe because it was Vermont, where people seriously believed in ghosts, or just because he looked like a man who knew darknesses at a time I was just inching up on mine, Miller Williams with his beard and piercing eyes looked satanic to me.

Conferences to critique our writing were scheduled for the second week, although I knew on the first day I'd been assigned to him. The theory was that after one week of classes, we'd understand much of the staff member's criticism. The reality was that each passing day increased our panic. His melancholy appearance did nothing to alleviate mine.

It's nineteen years ago and I see him clearly walking along the sidewalk toward our appointed meeting place. I jump up and run to catch up with him, and although he's somber and grave and I'm terrified, I attempt a joke. "In Michigan I'm known for my iron kidneys, but I've peed three times in the last half hour." He stops on the sidewalk, looks directly at me, and, without smiling, says, "You don't need to be afraid. You can do anything you want in writing." There were qualifiers, books I'd have to read, things I'd have to learn that'd take years, a lifetime, and I heard those other things he said, but they were all background music to the benediction he had pronounced: I had talent. Enough talent. We walked on. I was still afraid of him, but from then on, I thought of him—this is embarrassing for me and will be for him too, but it's how I thought of him then and think of him today—as savior. I was thirty-three years old with five children under eight with nothing going for me in writing except desire and obsession, and he told me I could be a writer.

Across a table, he handed me my poems. "Read through and then we can talk about anything you don't understand." Each page looked like a hemorrhaging bird had walked all over it. I finished and said, "I don't understand any of the marks." "We'll start at the beginning," he said.

> Let me tell you
> how to do it from the beginning.

He told me l.c. meant lowercase.

"Some of these poems are so terrible. And then every so often you do something like this . . ." He read a stanza aloud. Twice. "That is so damned fine. And to think that a housewife with five little kids is sitting in a house writing lines like that."

On my phrase "rural farmer" he said, "What else?"

"Good language here except for the underlined disasters."

He hated my bad puns.

"Don't settle for the nearly right word."

"Why did you use peanut butter cookies?" "That's what she brought." "Never confuse a fact with truth."

In a poem striving to tell a heavy secret, I used a fluffy image: "Don't trivialize your suffering. You must take yourself seriously. Your pain is legitimate."

"You have to be prepared to look up God's asshole."

"When you go home, you have to be ruthless. Gently ruthless but ruthless."

Later, when I was trying to tell him how much Bread Loaf had meant to me, he said I'd had "the Bread Loaf experience. Not a rebirth, but a birth. There are people who date their lives pre–Bread Loaf and past."

By now some of this may be fiction. Bread Loaf was one of the most important experiences of my life, but I never wrote anything down about it. It was too sacred, too terrifying. I thought I'd never forget it. Maybe I haven't, and Miller said all those things. I can only swear that these may not be the facts but it is the truth. The essence is: he was able to look beyond the bad and see the good and the possible. It strikes me now that that's the mark of a fine teacher, poet, and human.

I only saw him once after that, and it was an unhappy occasion: a meeting of high-powered writers where I felt shy, out of place, and downright miserable.

> I go out of the house for the first time
> since the day everybody found out
> and the first person I meet says hello turd

"I went from the Bread Loaf experience to the Hello Turd experience in just a few months," I wrote him after. He wrote back small comfort that took me years to grow into. "Well you know you didn't have to go into all the explanation. I understood and knew at the same time it wasn't for me to pull you into anywhere until you looked like you had your head down ready to roar in anyway."

I wrote him infrequently; I didn't want to impose. Yet eleven years after Bread Loaf, having long before switched from writing poetry to writing fiction, my first novel unpublished, my second rejected numerous times, in mounting agony that I was kidding myself, I imposed. I put my head down and roared in. "I want you to read the enclosed novel and tell me what you think." I knew that the blessing and curse of Miller Williams was that he always told the truth. His return letter, a praise, a validation, inspired me—filled me with the spirit—to continue until publication.

He's a master teacher, although his teacher poems are often about failure,

> but I will fail to tell you
> what I tell you
> even before you fail to understand
> so we might
> in a manner of speaking
> go down together.
>
> I should have told you something of importance
> ("The Associate Professor Delivers an
> Exhortation to His Failing Students")
>
> The students are sitting still in their one-armed chairs
> like rows of slot machines,
> most surely come to rest
> on the wrong combinations.
>
> I have not helped them very much.
>
> I love them. I tell them the truth . . .
> ("Paying Some Slight Attention to His Birthday
> the Associate Professor Goes About His Business
> Considering What He Sees and a Kind of Praise")

He never failed to tell me something because he always told me the truth. Going about his business, he made a difference in my life.

At Bread Loaf, Miller Williams may have looked like an old-time hellfire-and-brimstone preacher, but he also reminded me of a priest who, having committed every sin, finds it easy to give absolution. Compassionate, he never shies away from judgment. Witty and ironic, he never laughs at people. Unsentimental, he is remarkably domestic. The domesticity in his poems comes from minutely and honestly observed moments of living and love. As in "Husband."

> She's late. He mixes another drink.
> He turns on the television and watches
> a woman kissing the wrong man.
> He looks at his watch. He feels close
> to the cat. Well Cat, he says.
> He feels foolish.
> He mixes another drink and stands
> turning the stem of his glass
> back and forth in his fingers.
> This also makes him feel foolish.
> He looks at his watch. Well Cat, he says.
> Lights turn into the driveway.
> He slumps into his chair. He
> kicks off his shoes and spreads
> the open newspaper peacefully
> over his face.
> He hears the tiny grating of the key.
> His heart knocks to get out.

He can take you to school in death because he knows life in intimate detail. As he shows, for instance, in "And Then."

> Your toothbrush won't remember your mouth
> Your shoes won't remember your feet
>
> Your wife one good morning
> will remember your weight
> will feel unfaithful
> throwing the toothbrush away
> dropping the shoes in the Salvation Army box
> will set your picture in the living room
> Someone wearing a coat you would not have worn
> will ask was that your husband
> she will say yes

He knows not to sacrifice art to life or life to art: not many pull that one off.

When your father lies
in the last light
and your mother cries for him,
listen to the sound of her crying.
When your father dies
take notes
somewhere inside.

If there is a heaven
he will forgive you
if the line you found was a good line.

It does not have to be worth the dying.

I think he'd agree it'd have to be worth the living.

In "Notes from the Agent on Earth: How to Be Human," he writes about the privilege of discovering a devil in Rome:

In St. Peter's basilica in the City of Rome
there sits a holy father fashioned in marble
encircled by faces well-proportioned and doubtless.
His name is Gregory; he spoke for God.
He sits upon a slab; under that slab
the devil, winged and dog-faced, cat-pawed and crooked,
turns in his agony and bares his teeth . . .
. . . .
This loser, this bad and living dream, this Lucifer
alone is more than all the hovering others.
Because he carries folded into his face
what no face erased in heaven carries,
the fear and loneliness to make us human.
All there is to understand is there.

I had the privilege of discovering a devil at Bread Loaf.

 A Recollection

James Whitehead

It was a bad Gulf Oil map that got us lost somewhere in northwest Alabama that first time we were traveling from Nashville, Tennessee, to Columbus, Mississippi. This may sound like the making of an excuse for getting lost, but the more I recollect that spring weekend in 1958 the more clearly I see us in a cafe in Tuscumbia, Alabama, birthplace of Helen Keller, studying our map. We were studying very diligently while having coffee with our hamburgers, and smoking.

We're going to save a little time by way of leaving U.S. 43 near Hamilton—leave 43 and get on County 17 and go on down to Sulligent. Why we were looking for a shortcut is a good question. Sulligent, Vernon, Hightogy, then 96 and 50 into Columbus, where my sweetheart and wife-to-be was a senior at Mississippi State College for Women, where Miller was likely to sell some textbooks in his role as a college traveler for Harcourt-Brace. Miller also wanted to introduce me to a scholar who taught at the "W," The Brilliant Classicist.

What really happened was probably a confusion of Alabama 49 with County 17, because at no time in Tuscumbia did we foresee the Buttahatchee River. We took a wrong turn maybe, but the map, also, was deeply flawed.

We were going to take a shortcut for the hell of it, in order to vary our journey rather than to save time, to tell the truth. Maybe we were looking for Flannery O'Connor's Misfit—I'd met Miss O'Connor at a literary event at Vanderbilt, where I was in school. She read me the riot act because I asked her something about Catholic symbolism in her stories. She said there wasn't any. I'd been whopped by her the previous year, but recently Miller had become her friend. He was living in Macon, Georgia, and he'd gone to Milledgeville to pay her a call. They'd hit it off and he'd been there more than once. He'd seen the peacocks. He'd met her mother.

Peculiar things come to mind. This was my first spring away from football and during my first full season as a smoker. Miller was already and for many years an expert smoker, Old Gold Spin Filters. I enjoyed Pall Malls. When Miller lit a cigarette, he cupped his hands whether or not the wind was blowing. He'd push his shoulders forward and inward, and he used kitchen matches—often he did—or book matches. And he inhaled tremendously sometimes. I was a Zippo fan. I loved the heft of a Zippo, the weight of it in my pocket. Miller has been off cigarettes for going on twenty years. I've been off them for going on eight. He's a nonsmoker now. I'd like to fire up a Big Red this very moment.

We ate and drank coffee and smoked like fiends, then headed south and got lost around Hightogy or Guin, though probably it was an early version of Alabama 17. I was twenty-one or just twenty-two. Miller was twenty-seven. We're booming along in north Alabama being running buddies for the first time. The summer before this adventure was the summer I met both Gen and Miller. Miller was in fact with me when I first asked her for a date, and Miller had caught up with me in Nashville in the fall (I introduced him to John Yount, Bill Harrison, Bob Sorrells, George Core, and James Land Jones), but this was our first time on the road together, and that's important. Running buddies.

We're talking politics and poetry, E. E. Cummings or the Fugitives most likely. Miller liked Eliot and Frost well enough, Frost more than Eliot, as I remember, and he didn't care all that much for Yeats, but he took terrific pleasure from Cummings. I remember this because Cummings was not much taught in school and because I liked him even before Miller talked about the *beauty and intelligence* of Cummings's poetry. I praised Warren and Tate and Ransom and Davidson because I liked their work—though I had, and have, trouble with Tate—and because I'd been told to. Miller said you have to trust things that aren't fashionable, and he also said to count myself fortunate in attending a school that had produced excellent writers. He told me that in some way or another the Fugitives were our fathers. Miller had already published in little magazines. He was a poet for sure, and older. He could talk about literary fathers. I was very honored to be included in his sentence, honored to be his friend. I still am.

We turned off onto our shortcut and the sun was high. We're smoking with the windows rolled down. The blacktop has a line down the middle and we're talking Donne and Keats and Milton and Spenser. I'd taken Spenser in the fall and loved it. I enjoyed *The Faerie Queene* and was dazzled by "Epithalamion." Miller had read Spenser but was fonder of Milton. So was I. I was ravished by Milton. I was taking the course from Cyrus Hoy, a terrific course, but when Miller talked about Milton's *line*, I swear I must have confused him for a moment with Milton himself. Miller, beardless, looked a great deal like Hank Williams in those days. Miller also looked like John Milton about the time there was no longer a line down the middle of the road, about the time we zipped through what there was of Detroit, Alabama.

We'd go on about Keats and Donne in those days. I'd tell him I thought Donne was invented by certain professors and that the same people didn't pay enough attention to Keats and Wordsworth, and Coleridge. In junior high I'd memorized all or most of *The Rime* and still delighted in it. I had recently memorized "Kubla Khan."

Miller probably gave me a crooked smile, about the time the asphalt road began to break up and turn into a sorry dirt road. He, too, loved the *beauty* of Keats, liked Wordsworth and Coleridge, but I'll bet he put in good words for Donne. He is likely to have said something like, "I'll bet you that Donne turns out to be more important to your poetry than Keats." Smoke, Smoke. Magisterial inhalations. Hearing him say such a thing was like a calling. I'd recently left philosophy and theology for English, with hopes of writing, and I needed all the encouragement I could get.

And Miller had recently done something even more risky. What he had done seemed truly dangerous. He was an A.B.D. in physiology and had been teaching chemistry and biology in college for several years. He'd gone to college very young, and to graduate school. He'd loved science but had come to care more for poetry. He'd said, back in Nashville, "I'll never make a contribution to the field, in science. I know it. But maybe I can in poetry." *Contribution to the field*: I'd never heard any friend of mine put it that way. I was of course impressed. He had three children and a troubled marriage; he was poor as a church mouse. In fact, he was often broke; and he had changed jobs with a mind to get more money for his family, and in order to concentrate on writing poems. "I'll use the science, but I can't *do* science," he'd say. He was an older person.

We weren't slowing down, but the dirt road was going to hell on us right before our eyes.

"A good road is hard to find," I said.

"What the hell is going on?" said Miller, motoring along at a good clip, watching a hump rise in the center of our road, watching weeds begin to grow on the hump and in the tracks to either side of it. Except for a few houses in the little town miles behind us, there had been very few houses or shacks since we took the shortcut. The fields were fallow. You could see the old rows, old corn rows, among the sawgrass and bitterweed and dock, and there was a pretty good ditch beside each track. The weeds in the middle beat on the front of the Harcourt Chevrolet. They fluttered and crackled as they passed beneath the car. We passed a little side road, slightly less overgrown than our road, and headed directly for a line of trees that moved toward us like an unhappy predilection. You could say that. A birdcall was bright enough to cut through the rumble of the car, a note from some sweet world we were quickly leaving.

"*Stop* the car."

"Stop the *car.*"

A predilection and a premonition. The dust that had been running away from us came up to where we were standing. We're out of the car and staring at where the goddamned road goes into the trees—fine, ancient trees they were, too. Except for the hum of insects and the ticking of our Chevy's motor, there wasn't much to hear but these odd birdcalls from Paradise or the World of Forms and Intellectual Beauty. Never had flight seemed so desirable to me; and there was another sound, nearby but almost imperceptible at first, then growing louder as we stepped toward it, the sound of water, the sound of a pretty good river.

Miller pops his kitchen match with a longish fingernail, takes smoke to his heels. My trusty Zippo flashes in the last light before we walk beneath the limbs that are hanging over what is left of our outrageous shortcut.

"This peace has no place being on maps of any type," Miller said more ontologically than scientifically. He sucked his teeth and smiled. He was enjoying himself. He was making a contribution to the field, and so was I.

We knew. Never doubt it.

We knew there was a river, and we knew there was a bridge, and knew that the bridge was out, even before our eyes adjusted to the blue-green gloom beneath the trees. We walked right up to a concrete bridge that didn't look all that old. It was no iron rig with superstructure, old style. It was new enough, but the middle seventy or so feet of it had disappeared into thin air or into the swift little river that ran beneath it.

We were not talking much, and then Miller was pointing off to our left and toward the far bank downstream maybe forty yards, to where the back end of a sedan—four-door—was sticking out of the water. It was nose down, stuck into the bottom and also caught in a mess of tree limbs and heavy brush. Eddies curled away on the current side of that car. We were peering to see if there was a dead person in there. We were trying to see if we could smell one.

Whoever enjoyed the flight off the bridge, and the fall into the water, was gone and probably safe enough. They had long ago swum out—or had drowned and floated away.

Still, as I recollect, we called to see if anyone would answer. A snake fled across the water toward the other bank and time went on as usual. Snake doctors touched the water like anxieties.

And then we began to brood, even before we were back to the car.

Miller: "No sign at all."

Jim: "Sir?"

"There should have been a bridge-out sign."

"Right. But I'm glad it happened."

"I guess so," said Miller. "Yes!"

We didn't want to hang the car upon the corn rows, so Miller had to back up. Miller backed up in a hurry, using the rearview mirror and my instructions as I looked backward, my head out my window.

Finally we were back on a hard road with phone lines beside it, and there was a man walking along the side of the road as easy as you please. By this time Miller and I were puffing and cussing like tonk fighters. This wasn't literature, this was life. There was no excuse for having no signs of warning for a traveler. We were hot under the collar and late to see Gen and The Brilliant Classicist.

Miller pulled over and stopped so that our local stroller could come alongside us.

We'd pretty much decided that this fellow was the incarnation of backwoods Alabama. I rolled down the window and said to him, "That road back there, it leads to a road that leads to another road that runs up to a bridge that is out." I was straightforward but not obviously angry.

He stared down at me. He said, "Everybody knows *that*." But he was not vexed, and his gaze was mild.

"There are no signs of warning," Miller called from his side.

This tall Alabamian stooped to look across the front seat at the driver, but he never spoke another word before he went on his way.

At first we were chastened, and then we were convulsed, feeling largely delivered from all woe.

And then before long we were in Columbus, Mississippi, birthplace of Tennessee Williams and home of Mississippi State College for Women. I was excited to see Gen, but she had an afternoon class and so our visit together really wouldn't start until later. There we were on the springtime campus, azaleas flaming around the foundations of dorms and classrooms. The Brilliant Classicist (T.B.C.) came over, seeing Miller, and said, yes, he knew who Gen was but hadn't been introduced— "So nice to meet you, Gen and Jim." And would Miller and I come to his Latin class while Gen was in her class? His ladies were going to give a group recitation from Horace. He would appreciate it if Miller and I would read some of our poems afterward.

What a fine fellow he was. He told us how to get to his classroom and moved away quickly. Gen said she'd heard he was a wonderful teacher, and Miller said he was both brilliant and original. Gen was suddenly away to class herself, and Miller and I were moseying toward the odes of Horace and our reading.

"We didn't tell them about the bridge being out," I observed.

"You think they've heard about it already?"

And I told him that he could read *his* poems but I wasn't going to be fool enough to read after Horace and him. He asked, "Didn't you *bring* the poems?"

"Well, yes," I said. "So we could talk about a few if there's time."

"They're typed and in your black spring binder the way they ought to be? One must always be prepared to *read* if you're invited to. You've preached haven't you?"

"Well, yes. I wrote my last sermon in blank verse, the last one before I left the church last year." Which was true.

"Then you've already given a poetry reading."

By that time we were back at the Chevy. We got our binders and off we walked, poets.

Miller had told me that T.B.C. was a monarchist in the sense of wanting a king who would rule partially rather than absolutely. Jeffersonian democracy was a bit to the left but democracy was part of the tradition, and so on. Now Miller was and is a populist Democrat, the son of a Methodist preacher who was a founder of the Southern Tenant Farmers' Union, while my people were Ozark Lincoln Republicans who moved to Mississippi in 1940; not much room for a monarch in those positions, and I was a little bit amazed that Miller was so easy with the Classicist. In a fluttering of phoenix feathers, in the minute before Miller introduced him to Gen and me, they seemed to allude to ten books and twenty writers. This was the first time I remember hearing Robert Lowell called *Cal.* And I think that all this, including mention of two Civil War battles, was brought off with utter grace. *Red* Warren, *Cal* Lowell—my head was adrift as we found our way down the halls of a "W" building and, sure enough, incantations, decorous, solemn, and contemplative, flowed toward us from a door that was open down the hall a ways.

"Listen to that!" says Miller.

"Is he *really* a monarchist?" I asked.

"Listen up. Listen to the odes," he said.

When we got to the open door, T.B.C. saw us and waved off the recitation. *Click*—he seemed to have cut them off in mid-vowel, these attractive girls, about fifteen of them with their desks pushed together in order to read more or less chorally.

"Come in, come in," and we were introduced as Southern Poets. These girls were not so beautiful as Gen, but they were very pretty and had marvelous voices. After an injury during my freshman year, my football career had not been stellar, but here in this musty late afternoon classroom, because of what my host said by way of introduction, I felt the way I did when I made the All-Southern high school football team.

They recited for another ten minutes. Maybe fifteen. We sat in our classroom desks and were amazed. Then Miller read five or six good poems, and I read two or three that were not so good. The ladies were pleased. That's a fact. They clapped and then many of them shook our hands when class was over. Several knew Gen, and I hoped beyond hope that they would praise me and Miller for our performances. The Latin had *sounded* lovely. Miller's poems were not yet up to Tennyson's "Tears, Idle Tears," but I thought of them as being similar in mood and value to Tennyson's great lyric, my favorite poem at the time. I'd talk about other poets more than Tennyson, but "Tears" was the wonderful poem. My own stuff was metrically interesting, dramatically unclear, and, for the most part, metaphorically incomprehensible.

Miller, T.B.C., and I headed for The Goose, the college coffee shop, where we were to meet Gen, and it was during that walk, and over that coffee, before Gen showed up, that I experienced some dark thoughts, some forbidding premonitions. Mixed emotions, sinking feelings. Probably oxygen deprivation. I'm sure I was already well into my third pack of Pall Malls.

Gen would soon be coming to The Goose, this great beauty of her generation, whose destiny—and she knew it already—was to be the mother of many children. My children as well. I was determined to marry this extraordinary lady, and often this obsession left me confused, addled. And here were Miller and T.B.C. in high gear again. T.B.C. was talking John Crowe Ransom and Miller hung on every word—Ransom, who admired and feared science, hoping that nature and persons could be both understood (somewhat) and loved. Within a few years Miller would write a good book about Ransom—his favorite poem about that time was probably Ransom's "Winter Remembered." Ransom was the son of a Methodist minister and missionary to Brazil—Miller's father was a Methodist preacher—and these two poets, from that tradition, are as good as any two the South has produced. Yes, sir, Miller is now, in 1991, Ransom's equal in art. Warren is good, and Dickey, and others, to be sure, but Miller Williams is as good as anybody and ought to win the prizes. But he is, almost by nature, an outsider, brilliant, sometimes violent, genuinely humble, a good citizen of town, county, state and nation, and still and all an outsider, an Arkansan. Arkansans don't fit—God love them—and I was listening to Miller and the scholar debate the future of the South. Miller said that integration was the good news of the future; the Southern future would give the Negro the vote, and that would change everything for the better. (The first time I ever went to an integrated church service was with Gen at the little Catholic church in Columbus.) The scholar said that maybe we were right about all that, but watch out for the social engineers and the bureaucrats, the killers of ritual and myth, religion and poetry. The scholar said that he would not have us shot if his party came to power. All left-wing poets would be taught Spanish or Portuguese and sent to South America.

The Brilliant Classicist smoked Camels, I do believe, but casually and infrequently. Drinking coffee and smoking cigarettes, talking Art and Life at The Goose at the "W" in 1958, I knew I'd never be the same. We agreed to praise and repraise Mr. Frost, and to give high marks to Archibald MacLeish. T.B.C. and Miller thought of "You, Andrew Marvell" as wonderful. That poem struck me then, and strikes me now, as a busy poem but not quite wonderful.

I was thinking to myself, while Miller and the scholar were deciding on Ransom's best poem (Miller was willing to agree that "The Equilibrists" was close to "Winter Remembered")—thinking about a guy I'd met here in The Goose last fall, on my first visit to Columbus. Phil Luce, I think it was, and he was going off to join a revolution in Mexico. "Have you read *U.S.A.?*" he asked. I said, "No." He said, "Read it." I'd asked him didn't he think it peculiar to be seeing a "W" girl just before going off to join Zapata.

"If there was a revolution *here,* I'd join it," is what he'd said. Something like that. That guy went on to suffer the sixties in a big way is what I heard later.

That funny little room, The Goose, at M.S.C.W.—and here comes Gen in a Spanish skirt with several slips, and a bolero blouse.

Miller gave us the Harcourt Chevy for the rest of the afternoon and evening. The scholar told me where his mansion was, and of course he wanted Miller and me to spend the night there. Miller had said we'd be invited, so I said, "Thank you."

"Enjoy yourselves," he said as a blessing to me and Gen before we went off together.

In those days young women had to be in early, and so, after supper and a drive and a visit to the riverside, the Tombigbee River this time, I let Gen off at her dorm, telling her I'd be there in the morning, early.

God knows I'd had a good time with Gen, but it would be a lie to say I wasn't excited to see the mansion and to find out what they were talking about when I got there.

There was a full moon. I'd been enjoying it, and when I got to the address I'd been given, I could see that the great house was as handsome as I'd imagined, azaleas around it like fires around the feet of an elderly saint, you might say. White columns and porches above and below, she was an old beauty, and once inside I was not disappointed, for there were Miller and T.B.C., in the midst of a warm discussion concerning burial customs. Cremation or a wooden box? I was with our host on this one. I voted box. Miller voted cremation. The scholar's wife and children joined us, and soon we were all having a good time in the spacious hall that gave on to the sitting room on the right (facing in from the front door) and to what Miller and I were told was our bedroom on the left. Directly ahead was the big staircase that swung up to the left and to the rooms the family occupied. They were renting rooms in this building, watching over all of it as best they could, but is was pretty clear that the rent was low, that they were sort of camping out in this considerable relic. I was told that state and private funds would soon restore it for private or public use. The family was honored to be here for a while, and in the morning we could see the ducks in the room at the top of the stairs. The scholar said we'd get to see the ducks.

Miller nodded, but it was obvious that he had not yet seen the ducks. He bent to his cigarette.

There was no chandelier in that impressive hall, but what bulbs there were were bright enough, though not really bright at all. The hall was humid and dim, taken objectively, but the scholar's wife and children were lively, great fun. The children seemed to be able to hoot and holler and frisk around vigorously, running sometimes up and down the great stairs, without discouraging the adults in the least—which adults did not sit, as I remember, but stood around drinking toddies, large glasses full of Jack Daniels whiskey to be exact. The scholar would saunter here and there, patting his chaps on the head, telling a story about some kin or another at the battle of Franklin, telling Miller that he (Miller) ought to join the Church of England; be a socialist if you must, but be a Christian; telling me that Gen Graeber from Yazoo City was worth a world of care and that only the brave deserve the fair.

"Are you brave, son?" he asked of me. "You're going to have to be."

Miller was reciting snatches of Ransom and now and then breaking into verses of "I Saw the Light" and "Amazing Grace." The lady of the house was saying that Columbus was nice but it wasn't Nashville. We were all carrying on and then all of a sudden the scholar informed us that it was time for evening prayers.

"You gentlemen will join us, won't you?"

Of course.

And so—the scholar reading something from the *Book of Common Prayer*—we went to it, on our knees in that dim hall. Then the scholar prayed with his own words, then his wife, then each child, then Miller prayed and I prayed, all of it as pretty as you please. I believe we prayed for health and salvation, for peace, for friends and family, for poetry. Sure enough we did.

Voices were bickering in my head—"This is it, this is the future—time past and time future—you have bought a ticket for the whole tour. Is this the life of reason?" I regretted the loss of the locker room for a moment, and the pulpit.

I looked at Miller and saw that he was having a high old time. This man of sorrows was in a state of grace as we got up and went back to our drinks. This was my first serious experience with Jack Daniels, but my most vivid memory of that evening—my next-to-most-vivid memory—is of the children shouting and running up the stairs to bed, their pretty mother following. Portents. Voices of children echoing off the distant ceilings of those fine old rooms. The mother and the children disappeared from view, and the three of us were left in the hall below.

"What an excellent evening," said Miller.

"Wonderful," I said. "And I liked the Latin this afternoon."

"We've kept the children up late, haven't we?"—gesturing toward the stairs. The scholar seemed weary and seemed to be growing melancholy. "We'll have breakfast early. Gen will join us?"

"Yessir."

He knocked back his last swallows of whiskey and said that our bedroom was there—across from the sitting room. He pointed at it but did not lead us into it.

We followed him into the sitting room as he went to turn out the lights. Back in the hall he said, "There are fresh papers on the bed."

We heard him clearly.

Miller said, "Thank you."

I said, "Thank you, sir. We're fine." I was learning. He walked to the stairs, waved, and went up and away.

Miller looked at me with that wild, crooked grin of his. "Papers?" he said.

"Papers."

"What's going on?"

"Have you been into this room."

"No."

All of the above in whispers as we tiptoed toward it. For some reason, I clicked off the hall lights, and there we were in a large bedroom with only one piece of furniture in it. The four-poster in the moonlight. The full moon washed the room, entering through the several ceiling-to-floor windows—no drapes, no blinds, bare windows, a room awash in pearly moonlight.

On the bed were two complete Sunday editions of the *Commercial Appeal.*

"Jesus," said Miller.

"They don't look like they've been touched. You mentioned we might be coming, didn't you?"

"I don't think so."—Miller.

"Is he mad at us?—Is it a joke?"

"You got me. They're poor."

We got tickled. We were just about to break out laughing, but we didn't.

We got on the high old bed and spread some pages over us. I don't think we ever managed the papers very well. They didn't do for covers, or we didn't know what to do with them. I think there were pillows without slips, and Miller says he slept well enough, and I always do, whatever.

But before we slept, there was one further event of note. I was looking through the window onto the front porch, and sure enough there was a creature out there looking back at me. It was studying us and our papers.

"Miller, will you look at that," I said.

He gave the beast a long look.

"What is it?" he asked.

"It's a fox."

"Sure is a fox. It's a sign."

In the morning I went for Gen and told her about the newspapers, but there was no mention of newspapers from the scholar or his gentle wife. We saw the duck room, we had a very pleasant breakfast, and before long Miller and I had to take our leave of Columbus.

Late that spring Miller and I were back down there for a visit. The scholar was out of the mansion and into a cottage by the Tombigbee. We talked about that first visit at the mansion and I got around to mentioning the fox. This was our first mention of having seen a fox.

"Wonderful. I'm so glad you got to see the fox."

"By way of a full moon," said Miller.

"Best of all," said our host. "Best of all."

"Without the moon we'd lose our way, wouldn't we?" concluded Miller.

IV.

A POEM FOR EMILY

Small fact and fingers and farthest one from me,
a heart's width and two generations away,
in this still present I am fifty three.
You are not yet a full day.

When I am sixty three, when you are ten,
and you are neither closer nor as far,
your arms will fill with what you know by then,
the ~~word is~~ arithmetic and love we do and are.

When I by luck and blood am eighty six
and you are some place else and thirty three
believing in sex and god and politics
with children who look not at all like me,

some time I know you will have read them this
so they will know I love them and say so
and love their mother. Child, whatever is
is always or never was. Long ago,

a day I watched a while beside your bed,
I wrote this down, a thing that might be kept
a while, to tell you what I would have said
when you were who knows what and I was dead,
which is I stood and loved you while you slept.

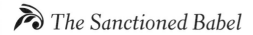 *The Sanctioned Babel*

An Interview
Richard Jackson

RICHARD JACKSON: In all your poems, however free they seem, there is a careful control of the line. Let's begin by talking about that basic unit, the line, about a theory of the line.

MILLER WILLIAMS: The line is very important to me. I like the five-stress line as a base, but I like to have it broken into twos and threes for sense, breath, conversational tone, pacing. If you take a poem like "The Caterpillar" or "Let Me Tell You," you can usually take adjacent lines and put them together into five-stress lines. I suppose, then, that almost all my poetry could be read as blank verse. But I hope that some interest is created when you realize that you are not moving through quite those blank verse rhythms. I hope that there's a tension between the sense of free verse and the sense of blank verse and that this creates a richness of texture. At least it seems to give me an opportunity to control pacing and meaning better than the squared blank verse base itself.

I agree with Conrad Aiken's 1917 review of *Prufrock and Other Poems.* He talked in that review about T. S. Eliot's fragmented blank verse, about Eliot's concealment of iambic pentameter. He suggested that this technique might be followed profitably in American poetry, and I think he's been proven right. And I think some of our best poetry has not only done that but has added "scattered" rhyme—full and slant rhymes that don't occur just at line breaks, but at more random intervals, unexpected places.

RICHARD JACKSON: Your poems have a very physical texture to them—not just by the metaphors and images you use, but through the sense of one level of discourse colliding with another, a sense of the abrasions and cuts in language. This is one way your lines form units. Could we relate this physicality of language to the use of sudden shifts and cuts, to a sense of surprise?

127

MILLER WILLIAMS: There ought to be continual surprise. I think a line should be a little poem; that is, I like for something interesting to happen in each line. The line break should not be arbitrary. I like a line to be a rhythmical unit and yet not be fully resolved in a rhythmical sense. When we say, "shave and a haircut, six bits," the phrase "shave and a haircut" is not a *resolved,* though it is clearly a rhythmical unit. We don't say "shave and a" as a satisfying unit.

I like a line to cause the reader to ask a kind of question and then have the question answered at the beginning of the next line. This creates a sense of forward motion. In the very simple terms of our small example, then, the line asks, "Shave and a haircut, what about it?" or "Shave and a haircut, how much?"

This forward motion is also carried by the sounds. When I write, I write out loud. It's very important to me how the consonants click off against one another and how the vowels move into one another and out again. I also like the sounds of a line to move in an interesting and logical way through the mouth. For instance, let's take the line, "Whose woods these are I think I know." You start with the center of sound just in front of your lips, and then it moves back low in your mouth, rocks up to the top of the soft palate, back down along the tongue, and finally out to the beginning point. There's an interesting sound migration there. It's like rocking back and forth on a rocking chair.

When the line does these things we've been discussing, I think a poem is going to have a sense of richness and texture. We can't make every line do all these things—it would be like eating fudge that's too rich. We couldn't deal with it. But maybe every line should strive to do these things.

RICHARD JACKSON: Roland Barthes talks about the physicality of language, relating it to what we might call the poem of pure play. He says, "The text of pleasure is a sanctioned Babel." You could also relate this "sanctioned Babel," I think, to your sense of irony—the way your poems lie "halfway" between the serious and the parodic, the objective and the subjective, the cold and the pathetic—the way one side of these dualities undercuts the other.

MILLER WILLIAMS: I think of most of my poems as having a touch of dark, hopefully ironic humor about them. I think there are many smooth and well-crafted poems that fail because of a lack of ironic vision. By the ironic vision, I mean that view of the world in which we see that all human statements contain their own contradiction and all human acts the seeds of their own defeat. Our acts, whether artworks, marriages, governments, whatever, are bound to fail because they are built upon the fallacious assumption that we can do what we set out to do, or that we can say what we mean to say. It's not important, for instance, that a husband and wife tell each other what they mean to tell each other precisely, successfully. It's important that they know they can't. It's important that when we set out to build the tower of Babel, and we don't get what we want, we find a way to live with what we get. I think this gives us a means to sanity.

RICHARD JACKSON: I'm reminded of your lines: "None of which facts we have gotten our words around, / not having understood them, words or facts. / We have been sure and courageous and skillfully wrong." There's a suspicion about language throughout your poetry, isn't there? And a suspicion about poetry itself?

MILLER WILLIAMS: Oh, yes. I'm concerned with our essential inability to know where we are at any given time, or to know what we're saying. Perhaps this is a poetic or humanistic version of the Heisenberg principle—the uncertainty principle. The thing we have to remember as poets is that we never get our words right. This is at least true in poetry. A Latin friend of mine once said that poetry is all "como si fuera"—it's all "as if it were." It's the same in our lives. We live life as if it were what we wanted; we read a poem as if it got to the truth of our lives. It never does, but the poet fails only because we all fail.

RICHARD JACKSON: "Think of Judas That He Did Love Jesus" is particularly interesting in the context we have been developing. In that poem you provide various versions of Judas that undercut each other. This strategy seems basic to all stories. In fact, you say, "These are the stories of Judas that fill the spaces / inside the story of Judas. Look quickly / behind the words you have heard and uncover creatures / looking the other way with words in their hands." There are always these "ghosts," *traces* that undermine history, story, gospel, conversation, perhaps even the poem. A question, maybe, of words and the Word. This raises the question of representation. Your poem "Cabbala," where there is a sense of a reality behind the dream behind the reality, raises the question in a more dramatic way.

MILLER WILLIAMS: Anything that we say in a poem has got to mean more than it would mean outside the poem, or the poem is not working. Poetry is an act of language that goes beyond the merely representational or the conversationally meaningful. The Judas poem tests out the implications of the fact that Jesus must have known what was going to happen, that he had to have someone there to betray him for the story's sake. This changes the usual view of Judas and so subverts the world order that the story represents.

But I want to say something about the suggestion in "Cabbala" that I question the objectively comprehensible universe. I don't mean to suggest utter chaos. I may seem to call into question an objective reality, but at the same time I write in a narrative framework filled with the furniture of this world. So when I question the reality of that furniture, I have to do this by building poems in which I assume that very reality. You have to start some place. What gets called into question is not the world itself but our ideas about it, our orderings of it.

RICHARD JACKSON: Precisely. And this explains the strong visual quality of your poems, doesn't it?

MILLER WILLIAMS: Well, I don't usually like poems that are purely contemplative. I like a poem to be a little short story. I'm reminded that Donald Justice sometimes says to his writing students when they show him a poem—"film it." It's occurred to me lately that a lot of my poems are cinematic—a kind of panning, zooming in and out.

RICHARD JACKSON: Well, there's another dimension besides this spatial, visual sense. I mean a sense of time. Of course, there's the man in "Notes from the Agent on Earth" who in a kind of Einsteinian universe invents a time machine to go back to his own childhood and kills the child and so has never lived to go back in the first place. We always see ourselves, you go on to say in the poem, standing in the past and talking to the people there. I suppose that raises the question of when and where we actually are. In "The House in the Vacant Lot," presence is seen as an absence, a ghost. And you give time a mythic dimension in "July 20, 1969"—as we go out to the moon, advancing technologically, we also retreat into a primitive past where the moon was worshiped.

MILLER WILLIAMS: You're the first person who's mentioned that—and I think it's important. I do play with time a great deal. I don't know if my concern for time is part of an aesthetic or philosophical position, but it is at least a problem in psychology. I can begin by saying that my concern with time originates with the uncertainty we were talking about before. We don't really know where we are in time or space; perhaps this is not *now* just as this is not *here*. Robert Penn Warren is another poet very much concerned with time, but our two concerns with it are like opposite sides of the same coin. For him, time is an unseen presence, but very real, that haunts his characters. I'm dealing with the problem of how we perceive time, and whether it can exist in a line or any sense of a "now" and a "to come." I think you're right in pointing to Einstein, and I'd point to Michelson and Morley, who also told us a lot about the illusory nature of time.

It may be that I'm using time as a synecdoche, then, as part of the illusory nature of the world. But in a poem you can't say everything is an illusion or there would be nothing to say. You have to find a particular something that's an illusion—time in this case—and let it represent the illusory nature of our perceptions, if not the world itself. I don't know precisely what I'm doing with time, but it intrigues me. I think I might come to say, though, that I do use time as a kind of synecdoche. I've never thought of that before.

RICHARD JACKSON: I wonder how much this sense of time can be related to the Calvinistic context of a poem like "Notes from the Agent on Earth," where you emphasize the terror of knowing how mortal we are. What makes us "human / . . . is a cold hand that reaches from under the bed" and closes on our ankles, the recognition that we may cross our hands on our chests when we sleep as we will in the coffin. And as you've been suggesting, this is part of the larger problem of just not knowing what will happen next. Perhaps, as you say in "How a Sparrow Was Caught in My Trap," the "darkness in our hearts is not what we think, / We ask how this could happen. We pretend. / The darkness in our hearts is that we know." What we know is a darkness.

MILLER WILLIAMS: The statement is ironic, of course. We know something, but the poem never says *what* we know. There is in all of us a secret darkness of the heart. It's a secret because none of us knows what is there, precisely. This is related, certainly, to Calvinism, and I think those who live in the Bible belt are more aware of it than other people. There's a certain guilt associated with this secret. Ultimately, I think my use of this religious background, and it is a strong background, is metaphoric. It doesn't finally matter what we call the source of our guilt, a godhead or whatever. Dealing with guilt requires me to deal with some sort of God-presence because that's the simplest way to introduce the question. We need a god for our guilt.

Still, I don't think I can talk very long about my poems in religious or Calvinistic terms because I think that if there is a pervasive statement in my poems, it is a humanistic one. A sense of guilt is a sense of isolation, and it's the sense of isolation that makes inevitable our sense of mortality, our sense of loss, our uncertainty about where and when we are, the consciousness of our illusions. Because of this isolation we try to build bridges between each other. This is what a poem does. This is a humanistic attitude, not a religious one. Perhaps the tone is colored by a religious background, but finally the important thing is the human being. My priorities are horizontal, not vertical.

RICHARD JACKSON: There's another aspect to this, related to your translating, which of course you do a lot of, and which you teach. I mean that the translator has to be able, as Keats says of the poet, to fill in for some other body; perhaps he has to have the same degree of "negative capability," too—the ability to live in uncertainty and doubt. The translator has to bridge the gap between cultures, doesn't he?

MILLER WILLIAMS: To me the role of the translator is very close to that of a spiritualist medium. When I'm translating I want the poet to be able to speak through me. I want to know his work well enough that I move from metaphor to metaphor at his pace, to vibrate as it were with him so that I can look at something and respond to it as he would. I want to create the poem that he would have created had English been his language. When we talk about the translator's humility, we're not talking about piousness, or even a humble deference, but the kind of humility that causes one actor to be quiet backstage when another one is working. Part of the humility is the awareness of the inability to say all we want to say, to say enough of what the original poet said. There's an essential futility, the futility of an act we can't help trying to perform. It's part of the terror of any writing, but also its motive.

 A *Descriptive* Chronology

Lyman Hagen

In a writing career spanning three decades, Miller Williams has produced eight volumes of poetry, numerous anthologies, textbooks and critical studies, several translations of foreign poets, short stories, and many articles. For this diversified and prodigious literary output he has won international recognition. Various reviewers have even suggested that he should already have won the Pulitzer Prize for his poetry.

Williams was born in Hoxie, Arkansas, on April 18, 1930, the son of E. B. Williams, a respected Methodist minister who served several congregations in Arkansas. Because ministers are often reassigned during a church career, the family didn't establish roots in any one town, though until Williams was grown he never lived away from his home state. Williams regards himself as both an Arkansan and a southerner, and his poetry reflects his identity. He's glad of his heritage and in a recent interview said:

> I don't love the South because it's good. I love it because it is whatever I am. I also have a real affection for the United States of America, but not because it's good. I have a deep love for my grandfather. You might not have called him good, but whatever he was I am. There's a kind of sham, a kind of smugness, in cutting yourself off from whatever you are. I either write out of my roots or I don't write. And these are my roots. I don't know what I would have done if someone had asked me before I was born, What roots would you like to choose? But I didn't choose.

After early semesters at Hendrix College at Conway, Arkansas, Williams graduated from Arkansas State University in Jonesboro in 1951 with a bachelor's degree in zoology. He then enrolled in graduate school and earned his master's degree in zoology and anthropology from the University of Arkansas at Fayetteville, thus acquiring the minimal academic credentials for teaching science in college, which he did for a number of years.

Eventually Williams became uncomfortable teaching science and decided it would be more honest to leave that task to others. "I was simply interpreting the text and not helping to shape the field," he has said. While searching for his niche, he turned to a variety of rather mundane jobs for support: traveler for a New York publisher; projectionist in a movie house; manager of a Sears-Roebuck furniture department; Montgomery Ward tire salesman; and stock-car driver.

In 1957 Williams won the first of many awards for his poetry, the Henry Bellaman Award. It was in 1961, however, that a major turning poet came in Williams's literary career: he met John Ciardi, the poet. Ciardi encouraged Williams and offered him the Bread Loaf Literary Fellowship for that year. (Later Williams spent seven years as a staff member of Bread Loaf.) At Bread Loaf Williams met Robert Frost; Dudley Fitts, who became a strong influence; John Frederick Nims; and Howard Nemerov. There at Middlebury, Nemerov and Williams often walked in the woods together, talking about poetry, and Nemerov offered to write the introduction to Williams's first book when it was published, a fact Williams recalled in a 1976 interview for *Poetry Now*.

In 1962 Williams decided to teach again and joined the English Department of Louisiana State University. Though he had no degrees in the field, the awards and recognition earned by his poetry gave credence to his natural talents.

Williams received the 1963 Amy Lowell Traveling Scholarship in poetry from Harvard University. He spent the 1963–1964 academic year as Visiting Professor of American Literature at the University of Chile, where he began translating Latin American poetry. In 1967, at Loyola University in New Orleans, Williams founded and edited the *New Orleans Review*. Rather than agree to university-imposed censorship at the magazine, he resigned, and in 1969 he accepted a Fulbright appointment at the National University of Mexico.

In January 1971, Williams joined the Graduate Writing Staff at the University of Arkansas. He became director of the Program in Creative Writing and for several years chaired both the Translation Program and the Comparative Literature Program. Williams was chosen to direct the newly established University of Arkansas Press in July 1980.

Williams published his poetry in collected form as early as 1951 in *Et Cetera*, a privately published chapbook. This was followed in 1955 by *Letters to the Editor and Other Poems*. About a decade later *A Circle of Stone* (1964), a collection of poems previously published in journals, initiated the new poetry series of Louisiana State University Press and was introduced, as promised, by colleague Howard Nemerov. Death and love are central themes in this collection.

Williams continued to turn out poetic précis: crisp, sometimes amusing statements about ordinary subjects, and these constituted *So Long at the Fair* (1968). More previously published poems were collected for his next book, *The Only World There Is* (1971). As the publisher's note indicates, it deals with "the world around us, of TV, war, racism, moon-landings." The fourth book, *Halfway from Hoxie* (1974), includes representative poems from the previous three books as well as new works.

After *Halfway*, Williams produced additional collections of poetry: *Why God Permits Evil* (1977); *Distractions* (1981); *The Boys on Their Bony Mules* (1983); and *Imperfect Love* (1986). An interesting feature of *Distractions* is the inclusion of translations from German, French, Spanish, and Italian (Romanesco) called "Parallel Lines."

Williams's latest collection, *Living on the Surface: New and Selected Poems*, was published in November 1989 by LSU Press. It was awarded the distinguished national award, the Poets' Prize, for 1990.

Williams produces actively in literary forms other than poetry: in *The Poetry of John Crowe Ransom* he analyzed the poetry of Ransom, and he has published stories and articles in a variety of anthologies. He is a translator of note: *Poems and Antipoems of Nicanor Parra* (1968), Parra's *Emergency Poems* (1976), and *Sonnets of Giuseppe Belli* (1981). He is founding director of the Translation Program at the University of Arkansas, as noted, and a past president of the American Literary Translators Association.

His several honors are testimonials that his poetic peers have recognized his talent. In addition to awards previously mentioned, he has won the New York Arts Fund Award for Significant Contribution to American Letters, the Prix de Rome for Literature presented by the American Academy of Arts and Letters, and numerous other honors.

Williams is the founding director of the University of Arkansas Press, which was established in 1980 and, after its first decade, has an annual list of forty titles. It has become one of the most prominent university press publishers of fiction, critical studies, and poetry. Among the writers on the list of the University of Arkansas Press are R. S. Thomas, John Williams, Ellen Gilchrist, Frederick Raphael, John William Corrington, George Garrett, John Ciardi, and John Clellon Holmes.

Williams continues to live and work in Fayetteville, Arkansas, where he has made his home since 1970. He divides his time among running the press, writing, teaching an occasional class, managing to keep his various languages current, and extensive travel.

David Baker has published two books of poetry, *Laws of the Land* and *Haunts*. He teaches English at Denison University.

Gabrielle Burton is the author of the nonfiction book *I'm Running Away from Home But I'm Not Allowed to Cross the Street*, and *Heartbreak Hotel*, a novel.

Fred Chappell's latest collection of poetry is *First and Last Words*. He is Professor of English at the University of North Carolina at Greensboro.

R. S. Gwynn is Associate Professor of English at Lamar University. His most recent collection of poetry is *The Drive-In*.

Lyman Hagen's complete bibliography of Miller Williams's work appeared in *The Bibliography Index*. He is Professor of English at Arkansas State University.

Richard Jackson edits *The Poetry Miscellany* and teaches at the University of Tennessee at Chattanooga. His latest book of poems is *Worlds Apart*.

X. J. Kennedy's most recent collection of poems is *Cross Ties: Selected Poems*. His textbook *An Introduction to Poetry* is in its seventh edition.

Maxine Kumin's latest books are *Nurture Poems* and *In Deep: Country Essays*.

Howard Nemerov served as Poet Laureate of the United States from 1988 until 1990. Winner of the National Book Award and the Pulitzer Prize, he was Edward Mallinckrodt Distinguished Professor of English at Washington University at the time of his death in 1991. His most recent publication, *A Howard Nemerov Reader,* includes selections from his work in poetry, fiction, and criticism.

John Nims's latest books are his *Selected Poems* and *The Kiss: A Jambalaya.*

William Stafford's most recent works are *Oregon Message* (poems) and *You Must Revise Your Life* (essays).

Lewis Turco is the author of *Visions and Revisions in American Poetry* and *The Shifting Web: Selected Poems.*

Robert Wallace is Professor of English at Case Western Reserve University. His new and selected poems, *The Common Summer,* were published in 1989.

James Whitehead is Professor of English and Creative Writing at the University of Arkansas. His two books of poetry are *Domains* and *Local Men.*

C. D. Wright is on the faculty at Brown University and is coeditor of Lost Roads Publishers. Her latest book of poems is *Further Adventures with You.*

✒ *Index to Poems Cited*